my **revision** notes

Cambridge National Level 1/2

HEALTH AND SOCIAL CARE

Judith Adams

HODDER
EDUCATION
AN HACHETTE UK COMPANY

Thank you to the Hodder team for their advice and editorial insight, especially Stephen Halder, Sundus Pasha, Alanna Burgess and all the other editors involved in the production of this book.

Love and thanks to Tony for his endless support.

Although every effort has been made to ensure that website addresses are correct at time of going to press, Hodder Education cannot be held responsible for the content of any website mentioned in this book. It is sometimes possible to find a relocated web page by typing in the address of the home page for a website in the URL window of your browser.

Hachette UK's policy is to use papers that are natural, renewable and recyclable products and made from wood grown in sustainable forests. The logging and manufacturing processes are expected to conform to the environmental regulations of the country of origin.

Orders: please contact Bookpoint Ltd, 130 Park Drive, Milton Park, Abingdon, Oxon OX14 4SE. Telephone: (44) 01235 827720. Fax: (44) 01235 400401. Email education@bookpoint.co.uk Lines are open from 9 a.m. to 5 p.m., Monday to Saturday, with a 24-hour message answering service. You can also order through our website: www.hoddereducation.co.uk

ISBN: 978-1-5104-2945-1

© Judith Adams 2018

First published in 2018 by
Hodder Education,
An Hachette UK Company
Carmelite House
50 Victoria Embankment
London EC4Y 0DZ
www.hoddereducation.co.uk

Impression number   10   9   8   7   6   5
Year   2022   2021   2020   2019

Cover photo © tai11/Shutterstock.com

Typeset in India.

Printed in Spain.

A catalogue record for this title is available from the British Library.

Get the most from this book

Everyone has to decide his or her own revision strategy, but it is essential to review your work, learn it and test your understanding. These Revision Notes will help you to do that in a planned way, topic by topic. Use this book as the cornerstone of your revision and don't hesitate to write in it – personalise your notes and check your progress by ticking off each section as you revise.

Tick to track your progress

Use the revision planner on pages 4 and 5 to plan your revision, topic by topic. Tick each box when you have:

- revised and understood a topic
- tested yourself
- practised the exam questions and gone online to check your answers and complete the quick quizzes

You can also keep track of your revision by ticking off each topic heading in the book. You may find it helpful to add your own notes as you work through each topic.

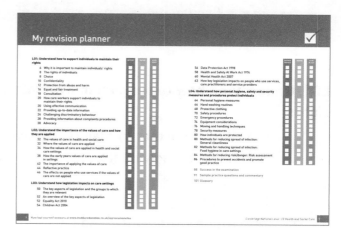

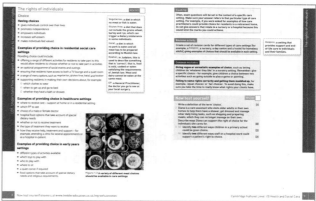

Features to help you succeed

My revision planner

REVISED   TESTED   EXAM READY

LO4: Understand how personal hygiene, safety and security measures and procedures protect individuals

L01: Understand how to support individuals to maintain their rights

Why it is important to maintain individuals' rights

REVISED

Everyone is entitled to rights. Rights are set out by **legislation** such as the Equality Act. (See LO3, page 52.) Practitioners who support individuals' rights will be working within the law and providing a high standard of personalised care.

Figure 1.1 shows the rights all individuals are entitled to. You can read more about these rights on pages 8–19.

Legislation: collection of laws passed by Parliament, which state the rights and entitlements of the individual. Law is upheld through the courts.

Exam tip

Learn the five rights. Make sure you can correctly name them all.

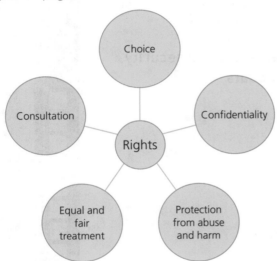

Figure 1.1 Individual rights

Revision activity

To help you remember the rights, use a mnemonic: three 'Cs and a 'PE':
- **C**hoice
- **C**onfidentiality
- **C**onsultation
- **P**rotection from abuse and harm
- **E**qual and fair treatment.

Figure 1.2 Why is it important to maintain individuals' rights?

Now test yourself answers at **www.hoddereducation.co.uk/myrevisionnotes**

Benefits for individuals when rights are maintained

- **High self-esteem** – this means a person feels valued and respected. High self-esteem is associated with people who are happy and confident. An individual with low self-esteem experiences feelings of unhappiness and worthlessness.
- **Empowerment** – this is to give someone the authority or control to do something. This is how a health, social care or early years worker encourages an individual to make decisions and take control of their life and become independent.
- **Confidence** –individuals will feel that they can rely on care workers and services to get high quality care that meets their needs.
- **Trust** – individuals must be able to feel that care workers are trustworthy, that they will not harm them and that they have their best interests at heart.
- **Safety** – care workers and care settings support individuals' rights to safety, will follow health and safety laws and ensure staff are trained in safeguarding procedures.
- **Equality** – individuals will be able to access the care they need. Adaptations will be made if necessary for them to access care.
- **Individual needs will be met** – individuals will receive appropriate care and treatment; for example, being provided with mobility aids, help with personal care or daily living tasks, medication or meal planning for a special dietary need.

Common mistake

Mixing up rights with the values of care. Make sure you know the difference. Rights are what individuals are entitled to; values of care are principles that underpin the care that is provided.

Now test yourself

TESTED ☐

1 Choose the correct answer from the list below. Which group of individuals is entitled to rights?
   (a) adults
   (b) babies and children
   (c) children, young people, adults
   (d) older adults
   (e) all of the above. [1]
2 Individual rights are set out by:
   (a) codes of practice
   (b) law
   (c) policies. [1]
3 Identify the **five** rights to which individuals are entitled. [5]
4 Give **four** reasons why it is important to maintain an individual's rights. [4]
5 Describe **three** benefits for individuals when their rights are maintained. [6]

The rights of individuals

Choice

Having choices

- gives individuals control over their lives
- promotes independence
- empowers individuals
- increases self-esteem
- makes individuals feel valued.

Examples of providing choice in residential social care settings

Providing choice could include:

- offering a range of different activities for residents to take part in; this would allow residents to choose whether or not to take part in activities
- an optional programme of social events and outings
- ensuring that residents have access to both a TV lounge and a quiet room
- a range of menu options, such as **vegetarian**, **gluten free**, **halal** and **kosher**
- supporting residents in making their own decisions about, for example:
  - which clothes to wear
  - when to get up and go to bed
  - whether they have a bath or shower.

Examples of providing choice in healthcare settings

- where to receive care – support at home or in a residential setting
- which **GP** to see
- choice of a male or female doctor
- hospital food options that take account of special dietary needs
- whether or not to receive treatment
- the type of treatment they want to receive
- how they receive help, treatment and support – for example, attending a clinic for several appointments or as a hospital in-patient.

Examples of providing choice in early years settings

- different types of activities available
- which toys to play with
- who to play with
- where to sit
- a quiet corner if required
- food options that take account of special dietary needs and religious requirements.

Vegetarian: a diet in which no meat or fish is eaten.

Gluten free: a diet that does not include the grains wheat, barley and rye, which can trigger a dietary intolerance in some individuals.

Halal: a diet in which no pork is eaten and all meat has to be prepared according to Muslim law.

Kosher: in Judaism, this is used to describe something that is 'correct'; that is, food is sold, cooked or eaten satisfying the requirements of Jewish law. Meat and dairy cannot be eaten at the same meal.

GP: a General Practitioner, the doctor you go to see at your local surgery.

Figure 1.3 A variety of different meal choices should be available in care settings

Exam tip

Often, exam questions will be set in the context of a specific care setting. Make sure your answer refers to that particular type of care setting. For example, if you were asked for examples of how care practitioners could provide choice for residents in a retirement home, do not give answers that relate to a nursery or a hospital because this would limit the marks you could achieve.

Revision activity

Create a set of revision cards for different types of care settings (for example, a **hospice**, a nursery, a day centre and a hostel for homeless adults), giving examples of choices that should be available in each setting.

Hospice: a setting that provides support and end-of-life care to individuals and their families.

Common mistakes

Giving vague or unrealistic examples of choice, such as letting children do 'whatever they like' in a nursery setting. Remember: give a specific choice – for example, give children a choice between two activities such as going outside to play a game or painting.

Failing to name rights correctly and getting them muddled up, for example, 'equal choices' or 'fair choices'. To avoid doing this, make sure you take the time to really know what rights your clients have.

Now test yourself

TESTED ☐

1 Write a definition of the term 'choice'. [1]
2 Diana is a care assistant who visits older adults in their own homes to help them have a shower, get dressed and manage other daily living tasks, such as shopping and preparing meals, which they can no longer manage on their own.
   Describe ways Diana can support the right of choice for the individuals she cares for. [8]
3 (a) Identify **two** different ways children in a primary school could be given choice. [2]
   (b) Identify **two** different ways staff on a hospital ward could support a patient's right to choice. [2]

Confidentiality

Care workers and practitioners have access to a lot of personal information about the individuals they are caring for. This information should be stored securely and only ever shared on a 'need-to-know' basis. Confidentiality limits access or places restrictions on sharing certain types of information so that it is kept private. The rights of individuals to have their information protected are set out in the Data Protection Act (see Learning Outcome 3, page 56).

Confidentiality is important because

- Care workers often receive very sensitive and private information from service users.
- Service users may be vulnerable and very trusting of those caring for them.
- It is unprofessional to talk about confidential matters outside of the care environment or so that others not involved in caring for that individual can overhear.
- It protects the interests of any individual, meaning that private financial or health information is not shared inappropriately with individuals who could use it to exploit or abuse someone.
- It helps service users to trust their carers.
- The service user's permission must be obtained before information is passed on to people outside the care team.

> **Need-to-know basis**: information is only shared with those directly involved with the care and support of an individual.
>
> **Confidentiality**: limits access or places restrictions on sharing certain types of sensitive information, so that it is kept private to only those who need to be aware of it.

Figure 1.4 Service users' personal information should only be shared on a need-to-know basis

Need-to-know basis

Sharing information on a need-to-know basis means:

- Information is only shared with those directly involved in the care and support of an individual.
- Access to the information is restricted to those who have a clear reason to access it when providing care and support for an individual.
- Telling a practitioner the facts they need to be aware of, at the time they need to know them to provide care for the individual, and nothing more.
- A practitioner can only pass information on to the relevant people. For example, if a teacher was concerned about a child's welfare they would tell the head of year, not all the other teachers in the school.

Care workers should always inform service users that they cannot keep all information secret and that sometimes it has to be shared with others involved in the individual's care. In certain, very specific, circumstances confidentiality has to be broken. See details of these circumstances in Table 1.1.

Table 1.1 Times when confidentiality has to be broken

When the individual ...	Examples:
intends to harm themselves	• person says they are going to commit suicide • person has mental health problems where they threaten to, or are, harming themselves
intends to harm others	• person threatens to seriously injure someone • person has mental health problems where behaviour puts others at risk of harm
is at risk of harm from others	• suspected child sex abuse • a case of domestic violence
is at risk of carrying out a serious offence.	• terrorism • drug dealing

Exam tip

Make sure that you understand the term 'need-to-know basis' and that you can give an example of it in practice.

Revision activity

Copy out Table 1.1 'Times when confidentiality has to be broken'. Cut up the table to separate the circumstances and the examples. Mix them all up. Correctly match the examples with the circumstances.

Common mistake

Stating that confidentiality means keeping everything 'secret'. Remember, care workers are not allowed to 'keep secrets'. All information relevant to the care of an individual has to be shared with all of the team caring for that person.

Now test yourself   TESTED ☐

1 Write a definition of 'confidentiality'.   [1]
2 Give an example of how a social worker might share information on a 'need-to-know' basis.   [2]
3 Give **two** examples of circumstances when confidentiality has to be broken.   [2]
4 Explain why confidentiality is important in care settings.   [3]

Protection from abuse and harm

All care settings need to follow safeguarding procedures to protect children and adults.

The Care Quality Commission (CQC) gives the following definition of **safeguarding**:

> 'Safeguarding means protecting people's health, wellbeing and human rights, and enabling them to live free from harm, abuse and neglect. It's fundamental to high-quality health and social care.'

> (Source: www.cqc.org.uk/what-we-do/how-we-do-our-job/safeguarding-people)

Procedures to protect care workers and service users from abuse and harm

All staff must:

- carry out **DBS checks**
- follow reporting procedures for abusive behaviour.

All settings must:

- appoint a **designated (child) protection officer**
- have clear and up-to-date:
  - complaints procedures
  - fire procedures
  - emergency evacuation procedures
  - lockdown procedures
  - policies on, for example, confidentiality, equal opportunities, 'no secrets'
- provide staff with training in:
  - **manual handling**
  - safeguarding
  - first aid
- hold regular fire drills (see LO4, page 72)
- carry out risk assessments of equipment and activities (see LO4, page 84)
- fully implement the Health and Safety at Work Act (see LO3, page 58)
- ensure high standards of hygiene in the care setting (see LO4, pages 64–7)
- ensure proper **security measures** are in place (see LO4, pages 78–9).

Individuals who are most at risk from abuse and harm include those who

- lack **mental capacity** – some people may be unable to tell others what is happening to them and may depend on others for decision making and getting their personal needs met
- have dementia – individuals with dementia may not realise that abuse is happening, or may have difficulty remembering and communicating
- have a learning disability – such individuals may not know what abuse is or understand their rights

Safeguarding: measures taken to reduce the risks of danger, harm and abuse.

DBS checks: criminal record checks carried out by the Disclosure and Barring Service (DBS), to help prevent unsuitable people working with vulnerable adults or children.

Designated protection officer: this person provides information and support to staff in care settings in relation to disclosures and suspicions of abuse. Early years settings have a 'designated child protection officer'.

Manual handling: using the correct procedures when physically moving any load by lifting, putting down, pushing or pulling.

Security measures: all the actions taken within a care setting to protect individuals; for example, procedures to ensure that only people with permission enter or leave the building.

Mental capacity: the ability to make decisions (by understanding information and remembering it for long enough) and communicate them to others.

Exam tip

Make sure you can give examples of procedures to protect care workers and service users from abuse and harm in each type of care setting – health, early years and social care.

- are in care – children who move in and out of different settings are less likely to develop trusting relationships with adults and may not know their rights
- have physical or **sensory impairments** – such individuals may be dependent on others and less likely to report abuse.

It is important to note that, just because the individuals listed above have extra needs, this does not mean they will all be unsafe or abused. It is just that the level of risk is increased – in other words, they are more **vulnerable** to being abused.

Sensory impairment: when one of the senses (sight, hearing, smell, touch, taste and spatial awareness) does not function normally. For example, if you wear glasses you have sight impairment; if you wear a hearing aid then you have a hearing impairment.

Vulnerable: someone who is less able to protect themselves from harm due to, for example, mental health problems or a physical or learning disability.

Abuse and harm is more likely to occur if

Staff are not trained properly in:

- how to use equipment, so may injure themselves or those who are in their care; for example, when transferring someone out of a bath using a hoist
- manual handling, so may injure someone they are caring for or themselves; for example, when moving a service user from a bed to a chair
- correct procedures when providing intimate care, such as bathing, changing incontinence pads and so on, so may be accused of abuse
- diversity and equality, so incidents involving **prejudice** and **discrimination** are more likely to occur
- safeguarding procedures, and so are unaware of their role in dealing with suspected abuse or harm.

In addition, abuse and harm are more likely to occur if:

- staff are not DBS checked, meaning it is not known whether they have a criminal record and have been barred from working with vulnerable adults and children, so putting the individuals in their care at risk
- there is a shortage of staff, meaning staff are rushed and may neglect service users due to lack of time, or may get impatient, for example, if someone with dementia is taking 'too long' to get dressed.

Finally, it is important that staff carry out careful checks of:

- equipment, such as hoists, toys – if these are old and/or damaged they could cause injury
- activities and visits – these need to be risk assessed so potential hazards and ways of avoiding them are identified.

> **Prejudice**: a dislike of, or negative attitude towards, an individual often based on ill-informed personal opinion. Examples include racial prejudice and homophobia.
>
> **Discrimination**: the unjust and unfair treatment of individuals based on their differences, such as race, religious beliefs, disability or gender.

Figure 1.5 Staff training is essential to avoid injuring service users or care workers when using a hoist

Now test yourself answers at www.hoddereducation.co.uk/myrevisionnotes

Revision activity

Create a concept map for this topic. It should cover the main information relating to:

- procedures to protect care workers and service users from harm and abuse
- individuals who are most at risk from abuse
- when abuse and harm are more likely to occur.

Common mistake

Not using the correct terminology for this topic. In order to gain the highest marks, make sure you know what terms such as safeguarding, manual handling and mental capacity mean and use them accurately.

Now test yourself

TESTED

1 Identify **four** procedures that would help to reduce the risk of abuse and harm in a care setting. [4]
2 Identify **three** individuals who may be at greater risk of abuse or harm when in a care setting and give a different reason why for each. [6]
3 What do the initials DBS stand for? [1]
4 How does the DBS ensure that an individual is suitable to work with children or vulnerable adults? [3]

Equal and fair treatment

Equal treatment means being given the same opportunities and choices as everyone else.

Fair treatment means being able to have full access to those opportunities and choices, as well as receiving the type of care that meets individual needs.

Example 1

Staff at a residential care home for older adults have arranged a day trip to the coast for all of the residents who want to go. The coach that is taking the residents on the trip must have a wheelchair ramp, otherwise those residents who are wheelchair users will be unable to go.

Figure 1.6 Providing a wheelchair ramp enables access

Example 2

It is important that children with **special educational needs** can take part in the same lessons as the rest of their class. This ensures equality of opportunity. Without extra support, a child with special educational needs might struggle with the class work, which would not be fair treatment.

Children with special educational needs can be enabled to stay with their class if they are given extra support, such as differentiated worksheets and tasks. This might include one-to-one support from a teaching assistant who could, for example, act as a translator or use sign language.

In this way, being treated differently ensures the child has equal opportunities.

> **Special educational needs:** children with learning or physical disabilities, for example, hearing or visual impairments, or conditions such as ADHD or autism.

Individuals using health, social care and early years services should be treated in accordance with the Equality Act (see LO3, page 52) and in such a way that their individual needs are met, as shown by the two examples above.

Equal and fair treatment means individuals are

- given the same opportunities and choices
- treated for their individual needs.

It does NOT mean individuals are:

- treated unfairly
- discriminated against.

Remember, treating people fairly means treating them in the way most appropriate to their individual needs. This may mean care workers treat some individuals differently than others, because different people have different needs. For example, a teaching assistant may give a child help with reading on a one-to-one basis while the rest of the class is taught as a group. The child having one-to-one help is being given special treatment and support to enable them to catch up and develop the same level of skills as the rest of the class.

Figure 1.7 Providing extra support in the classroom

Exam tip

Learn the definition of 'equal' and 'fair' treatment.

Revision activity

For health, social care and early years services try to think of three examples **each** where individuals are treated differently in order to ensure they have equal opportunities.

Now test yourself

TESTED

1 Explain the difference between 'equal treatment' and 'fair treatment'. [2]
2 How does a nursery providing a wheelchair ramp support individuals' rights? [2]
3 What is the most important piece of information a care worker should remember about the person they are caring for?
   (a) their e-mail address/phone number
   (b) whether they are Muslim, Jewish or Christian
   (c) that they are an individual
   (d) their age. [1]

Common mistake

Stating that 'treating everyone the same' is equal treatment. People have to be treated in line with their individual needs. Remember: different individuals have different needs.

Consultation

It is important that individuals are consulted and involved in the decision-making process for their own care and support. This requires service users to work in partnership with the practitioners providing their care and the relevant support services. **Consultation** could take place directly with the service users themselves or through a service user's representative, such as a family member, friend or **advocate**.

> **Consultation:** the process of discussing something with someone in order to get his or her advice or opinion, so that a decision can be made that is acceptable to all involved.
>
> **Advocate:** someone who speaks on behalf of an individual who is unable to speak up for him or herself.

Figure 1.8 Aspects of consultation

Ways practitioners can support an individual's right to consultation

- Ask for their opinion.
- Listen to their views.
- Ask what type of care they would like, if it were possible.
- Give information about the options available to them.
- Provide information about different treatments and explain their benefits and disadvantages.
- Explain what different treatment options will involve.
- Share decision making based on the individual's opinions.

> **Common mistake**
>
> **Mixing up the rights of 'choice' and 'consultation'.** Make sure that you know the difference. Remember that choice means to select from options you have been given, while consultation means discussing and exploring possible options.

How consultation supports rights

Consultation means seeking the individual's views and opinions so their personal preferences can be taken into account, informing their choice of care provision. This means individuals feel:

- valued and listened to
- in control
- empowered to make an informed choice
- confident that the care meets their individual needs.

Figure 1.9 Getting to know an individual

Exam tip

Make sure you can give examples of consultation for practitioners in health, social care and early years settings. Exam questions are often based on a particular setting such as a primary school, GP surgery or residential care home.

Revision activity

Figure 1.9 shows a care worker having a discussion with a resident of a retirement home. Make a list of questions that the care worker could ask to support the resident's right to consultation

Now test yourself

TESTED ☐

1 Write a definition of 'consultation'. [1]
2 List **four** features of consultation. [4]
3 Identify **two** ways a practitioner could support an individual's right to consultation. [2]
4 Explain how a hospital doctor could support a patient's right to consultation regarding their treatment. [5]

How care workers can support individuals to maintain their rights

Using effective communication

Verbal and non-verbal communication

Communication is a two-way process of sharing messages using both verbal and non-verbal methods.

- Verbal communication is what we say to another person.
- Non-verbal communication is using **body language**, written or specialist methods of communication.

Effective communication skills by care workers will ensure that messages are understood.

Table 1.2 How to communicate effectively

Use vocabulary that can be understood	• no **jargon** • explain specialist terminology • use age-appropriate vocabulary • simplify language; for example, when speaking with young children, individuals with learning disabilities or patients with dementia • use **interpreters** or **translators**, where necessary.
Don't be patronising	• use positive body language; for example, smiling, nodding to show agreement, relaxed posture • avoid sarcasm/talking down to the person • be polite and show respect through active listening • take what the person has to say seriously • be patient when listening to repetitions • do not ignore a person's views or beliefs because they are different to yours.
Adapting your communication to meet the needs of the individual or situation	• emphasise important words • slow down to speak at a clearer pace • vary the **tone** of your voice; for example, speak more loudly to support hearing but avoid shouting, or to be discrete, quietly ask a care home resident whether they need to go to the toilet • repeat phrases where appropriate and check understanding • use gestures where helpful • make use of aids to communication, such as loop system, flash cards, specialist methods such as Braille, signing, **PECS**, technological aids such as **Dynavox** and **Lightwriter**.
Listening to individuals' needs	• use active listening – demonstrate interest in, and respond to, what a person is saying • concentrate on what the person is saying – this will encourage them to communicate their needs • use body language to show a positive reaction, such as nodding your head • ask the person – do not assume you know what they want, need or prefer.

Body language: a type of non-verbal communication through body posture, facial expressions, gestures and eye contact.

Jargon: specialist or technical language or terms and abbreviations that are difficult for non-specialists to understand.

Interpreter: converts a spoken or signed message from one language to another.

Translator: converts a written message from one language to another.

Patronising: talking down to someone, as though they were a child or simple-minded.

Tone: the strength of a vocal sound made, for example, quiet or loud.

PECS: Stands for 'Picture Exchange Communication System'. It is a specialist method of communication developed for use with children who have autism. It helps them learn to start communicating by exchanging a picture for the item or activity they want.

Dynavox: speech-generating software. By touching a screen that contains text, pictures and symbols, the software then converts those symbols touched into speech.

Lightwriter: a text-to-speech device. A message is typed on a keyboard, displayed on a screen and then converted into speech.

How using effective communication supports rights

- it aids understanding of procedures/treatment/what's happening, and so on
- the individual feels valued
- it instils confidence
- it develops trust
- it shows respect
- it shows that you are listening
- the individual feels they are being taken seriously
- it enables informed decisions/choices to be made
- it provides equality of access
- it empowers individuals
- it raises self-esteem
- it helps to meet the individual's needs.

Exam tip

You should be able to suggest ways of communicating effectively with a range of different service users, including young children, those with learning difficulties, individuals who are blind or hearing impaired, people who do not speak English, those who are upset and distressed and older people with dementia, as well as other care workers in the setting.

Revision activity

Look carefully at Figure 1.10. Identify the verbal and non-verbal communication skills the care worker is using. Explain how the skills you have identified demonstrate effective communication.

Common mistake

Confusing an interpreter or translator with someone who uses sign language. Make sure you know the difference! Interpreters and translators convert from one language to another. Sign language is using specific gestures to communicate with someone who is hearing impaired.

Figure 1.10 Using effective communication skills

Now test yourself

TESTED ☐

1. Give **two** examples of non-verbal communication and **two** examples of verbal communication. [4]
2. Describe **two** ways of communicating effectively with an individual who has dementia. [4]
3. Explain how effective communication supports individual rights. [5]
4. Suggest **two** ways a Practice Nurse could communicate effectively with a patient who only speaks Polish. [4]

Providing up-to-date information

To support individual rights, it is important that health, early years and social care settings provide service users with up-to-date information. This is because having knowledge and information empowers individuals and enables them to make informed choices.

Table 1.3 gives some examples of different types of information and how access to this information supports individuals' rights.

Table 1.3 How accessing up-to-date information supports individual rights

Information	How accessing up-to-date information supports individual rights
Opening and closing times of services	<ul><li>means individual knows when they can access services</li><li>they won't waste time attending when services are not available</li></ul>
Contact details for the service (address, phone numbers and e-mail)	<ul><li>providing up-to-date contact information enables individuals to communicate with the service provider</li></ul>
Names of staff and their job role	<ul><li>individuals know which person to ask for</li><li>individuals feel more confident they are speaking to the correct person for their needs</li></ul>
Type of care services provided	<ul><li>the individual can choose what type of service is most appropriate for their circumstances; for example, at home with support or in residential care</li><li>supports individuals to make informed choices</li></ul>
Location of services	<ul><li>means individuals who need care and support are aware of where specific services are available locally and nationally</li></ul>
Alternatives available	<ul><li>knowledge empowers individuals to take control of their own decisions</li><li>the individual can choose what type of care or treatment is most appropriate from the options available: for example, the option to attend counselling sessions for a condition such as depression, or medication, or a combination of both</li></ul>
Results of tests/treatments/ progress report	<ul><li>means that individuals know why they are in need of treatment or care</li><li>individuals can be informed about the options for treatment or care that will be required</li></ul>
Complaints procedures	<ul><li>individuals will know what to do and who to speak to if their rights or needs are not being met</li><li>reassures service users that their concerns will be taken seriously.</li></ul>

Exam tip

Exam questions may require examples of up-to-date information that link to a particular setting, such as a hospital, a playgroup or a day centre. Make sure that you know some examples of up-to-date information for each of the three types of setting: health, social care and early years.

Now test yourself

TESTED ☐

1   Identify **three** additional pieces of information that are needed on this health centre sign to make it more useful for patients.   [3]

> **Greenacres Health Centre**
>
> **Opening times:**
>
> **Monday – Friday**
>
> **Session 1 – morning**
>
> **Session 2 – afternoon**
>
> **Please contact us if you require an appointment**

2   Identify four pieces of up-to-date information a nursery could provide for parents.   [4]

3   Explain how a nursery providing up-to-date information supports the rights of children and their parents.   [6]

4   Outline the up-to-date information a patient would require when they are discharged from hospital after having had an operation.   [5]

Challenging discriminatory behaviour

Discriminatory behaviour can involve

- treating someone unfairly or less favourably compared to others
- excluding someone from activities
- verbal or physical abuse.

Discriminatory behaviour from care workers can result in abuse, **neglect** or inadequate care of individuals using care services for help and support.

> **Neglect**: fail to look after properly.
>
> **Breach**: breaking the law; not meeting the requirements.

Table 1.4 Examples of discriminatory behaviour

Prejudice	<ul><li>A nurse is reluctant to attend to patients from different ethnic backgrounds to her own.</li><li>A nursery nurse thinks that children from a certain postcode are 'common' and treats them less favourably than others.</li></ul>
Inadequate care	<ul><li>A childminder sits a child in front of the television all day to keep them quiet.</li><li>Hospital patients' physical needs are neglected; for example, having to wait many hours for food and drink, or not being taken to the toilet in time.</li></ul>
Abuse and neglect	<ul><li>Verbal abuse, such as day centre staff mocking and making jokes about young adults with learning disabilities.</li><li>Care assistants causing bruises by handling residents roughly while giving them a bed bath.</li><li>A residential home for adults with dementia not providing any activities for the residents because 'there is no point, they won't remember anything'.</li></ul>
Breach of health and safety laws	<ul><li>A care setting not having any trained first aiders so immediate treatment is not available.</li><li>A member of staff not trained in manual handling causes injuries to a service user when using a hoist.</li><li>Equipment is not regularly checked for damage so children in a nursery cut themselves on a damaged toy.</li><li>Inadequate hygiene practices put residents in a care home at risk of food poisoning.</li><li>Activities are not risk assessed, increasing the chance of someone having an accident.</li></ul>

Three main ways to challenge discriminatory behaviour

Incidents of discriminatory behaviour in care settings, whether by service users or care workers, should always be challenged with an appropriate action.

1: Challenge at the time

- Explain to the individual how they are being discriminatory to raise their awareness of what they are doing and how it is inappropriate.
- Make the person reflect on their actions – what they have done or said – and ask them to consider what they would do in future.
- A more senior member of staff could supervise the person so that their work with service users can be monitored.

2: Challenge afterwards through procedures

- Refer the person to the setting's policies; for example, equal opportunities, bullying.
- A senior member of staff could be consulted for advice and discussion of how to deal with the issue.

Now test yourself answers at **www.hoddereducation.co.uk/myrevisionnotes**

- In a serious case, **disciplinary action** could be taken against the member of staff – this will make them aware of the seriousness of what has happened and provides a basis for changing their attitudes.
- Implement complaints procedures – this means that people using the service are aware of how to take action if they have a complaint about discrimination or poor practice.
- **Whistle blowing** – in exceptionally serious situations, this involves raising concerns about poor practice with the person in charge of the setting at the very highest level or with an outside authority such as the Care Quality Commission or Ofsted. They will carry out an investigation and take appropriate action, which could involve prosecuting staff or closing down the care setting.

Disciplinary action: a member of staff may be given a warning, or suspended, or – in very serious circumstances – dismissed because of not doing their job properly to the required standards.

Whistle blowing: when someone reveals serious wrongdoing within an organisation to an outside authority such as the Care Quality Commission, so that it can be investigated.

3: Challenge through long-term proactive campaigning

- Equality and diversity awareness sessions could be provided for the person discriminating and all staff on a regular basis, to ensure they are fully aware of what discriminatory behaviour is, why it is unacceptable and how to avoid it.
- Provide staff with training in effective communication.
- Send the person who has discriminated on an anger management course.
- Provide staff with regular training over time to raise awareness of the correct ways of working so they know how to respond if they observe discriminatory practice.

Proactive: taking action intended to cause changes rather than just reacting to the situation after it has happened.

Figure 1.11 Equality and diversity training session for hospital staff

Exam tip

If you are asked to explain a way of challenging an individual's discriminatory behaviour, you need to provide a specific and detailed explanation. Suggesting something like 'put up anti-bullying posters' is unlikely to have much impact, as people may not read them. A better response would be: 'arranging an anti-bullying information session for all staff which includes going through the setting's bullying policy. The session could be supported by giving all staff in attendance an information leaflet to keep and by putting up anti-bullying posters that include guidance on what to do if you observe or experience bullying behaviour.'

Revision activity

For each of the examples of discriminatory behaviour given in Table 1.4, explain how the behaviour could be challenged.

Common mistake

Giving vague answers such as 'tell them it is wrong' when asked for an example of how to challenge discriminatory behaviour. You need to give a specific example and explain how this will have an impact on, and change, the person's behaviour. For example, you could say 'Speak to them at the time and tell them that what they have done is inappropriate and why. This will help them to understand how to change their behaviour so it is not discriminatory.'

Now test yourself

TESTED [ ]

1 Identify **two** ways of challenging a colleague who makes discriminatory comments about older people using a care setting. [2]
2 Discuss ways a manager could challenge a member of staff who has been discriminating against patients from ethnic minority groups. [5]
3 Explain the meaning of 'long-term proactive campaigning'. [3]

Providing information about complaints procedures

A care setting that provides information about complaints procedures

- enables all individuals in a care setting – staff, service users and their families – to take action against poor care or treatment
- empowers individuals to seek **redress** to correct a situation or put things right
- protects individuals from discrimination, abuse and unfair treatment.

> **Redress**: to obtain justice after receiving inadequate care. This may take the form of compensation awarded by the courts or having your rights restored in some way.

When to complain

When rights have not been met; for example:

- a care home resident:
  - is not given any choice of what to wear, activities or meals
  - can have a shower or bath only twice a week
- confidentiality has been broken unnecessarily
- a service user is injured in the setting when being moved with a hoist
- incorrect medication is provided to a service user
- a hospital patient is discriminated against due to age, race or gender
- treatment or care decisions are made without involving the service user.

Options when making a complaint

When making a complaint, you will need to consider the following.

- Is the complaint formal or informal? For example, is it necessary to write a formal letter of complaint or would an informal conversation be sufficient?
- When to make the complaint – straightaway or later? For example, you may wish to discuss the problem with senior staff or a manager first.
- Who to complain to – the member of staff, a supervisor, the management or the owner of the setting?
- Whether to take up the issue with external services, for example, the police, a solicitor, the local health authority, the Care Quality Commission, Ofsted, the Equality and Human Rights Commission.

Steps to take when making a complaint

Sometimes an individual may decide not to make a complaint; for example, because they:

- don't want to make a fuss
- are worried that doing so might be stressful
- might lack sufficient evidence to prove what happened
- don't know who to complain to
- don't know the procedure to make a complaint
- are worried they will not be believed.

Procedures to follow when making a complaint

- Follow the steps of the setting or service's complaints procedure.
- Act on the professional advice you have been given about the best way to make the complaint.

Now test yourself answers at **www.hoddereducation.co.uk/myrevisionnotes**

- Provide a clear description of what happened.
- Share any evidence you have gathered.

Complaints procedures enable

- individuals to openly raise concerns and complaints
- care settings to review complaints received, to monitor the quality of the care they provide
- care settings to highlight action they need to take to improve the quality of care they provide
- settings to show they are striving to promote good practice by responding promptly to complaints
- trust and confidence to be established, as service users know their views and opinions are taken seriously.

Exam tip

Make sure you can give specific examples of when to complain, how to complain and the procedures to follow.

Revision activity

Write a list of advice for a friend who feels they have been the victim of poor treatment by their GP surgery. Provide them with step-by-step instructions of what to do if they wish to make a complaint.

Common mistake

Not being able to produce a list of steps to take when making a complaint. Don't just write 'see someone in charge and complain'. You need to give specific steps, such as 'write down what happened, ask any witnesses to do the same, find out about the setting's complaints procedure and then speak to the person in charge'.

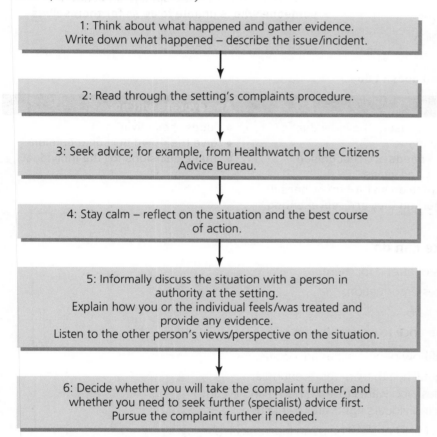

1: Think about what happened and gather evidence. Write down what happened – describe the issue/incident.

2: Read through the setting's complaints procedure.

3: Seek advice; for example, from Healthwatch or the Citizens Advice Bureau.

4: Stay calm – reflect on the situation and the best course of action.

5: Informally discuss the situation with a person in authority at the setting. Explain how you or the individual feels/was treated and provide any evidence. Listen to the other person's views/perspective on the situation.

6: Decide whether you will take the complaint further, and whether you need to seek further (specialist) advice first. Pursue the complaint further if needed.

Figure 1.12 **Making a complaint**

Now test yourself

TESTED

1 Explain the meaning of the phrase 'to seek redress'. [1]
2 Describe **three** examples of situations where an individual should make a complaint: one for a nursery, one for a hospital and one for a residential care home. [3]
3 Identify **three** reasons why an individual may decide **not** to make a complaint. [3]
4 Explain how a care setting supports individual rights by having a complaints procedure. [5]

Advocacy

Health, social care and early years services can support certain individuals' rights by providing an advocate.

Who might need an advocate?

- A young child.
- An individual with a learning disability.
- An older person with a condition such as Alzheimer's.
- Someone who has been assessed as lacking mental capacity.
- People with mental health problems.
- An individual with a physical disability.

Figure 1.13 An advocate speaks on behalf of someone who is unable to do so for themselves

Table 1.5 What an advocate does and doesn't do

An advocate will:	An advocate will not:
<ul><li>be completely independent and represent the individual's views, not their own personal opinions</li><li>ensure an individual's rights and needs are recognised</li><li>represent the individual's wishes and views</li><li>speak for someone who is unable to do so for him or herself</li><li>act in the best interests of the person they are representing.</li></ul>	<ul><li>judge the individual</li><li>give their own personal opinion</li><li>make decisions for the individual.</li></ul>

Examples of what an advocate can do

- Go with an individual to meetings or attend for them.
- Help an individual to find and access information.
- Write letters on the individual's behalf.
- Speak for someone at a case conference to express their wishes.

Consider these different examples of how people act as advocates.

- A member of the community mental health team representing an 18-year-old with learning difficulties who wants to leave home and live in supported housing, to ensure the individual's rights are maintained.
- A volunteer from a charity such as MIND or SEAP helps an individual with an application for disability benefits, to ensure the individual's rights and entitlements are supported.
- A family friend represents an older person with dementia by speaking about their needs with a hospital social worker when a care plan is being discussed, to ensure their best interests are supported.

Advocacy supports and enables people to

- express their views and concerns
- have their voice heard on issues that are important to them
- access the information and services they need
- defend and promote their rights
- explore choices and options for care and/or treatment
- have their views and preferences genuinely considered when decisions are being made about their lives.

Revision activity

Draw a 4 × 4 grid with four rows and four columns. Fill in each cell with a fact about advocacy.

Exam tip

Make sure that you can write a definition of advocacy and can give an example of how it can support an individual's rights.

Common mistake

Stating that advocates 'speak for' someone. This is inaccurate. Advocates represent the views and preferences of an individual – they speak on their behalf, not 'for' them.

Now test yourself

TESTED ☐

1 Give an example of a situation where a young child might need an advocate. [1]
2 Give **three** practical examples of what an advocate could do when representing someone. [3]
3 How does advocacy support an individual's rights? [3]

LO2: Understand the importance of the values of care and how they are applied

The values of care in health and social care

REVISED

These are:

1 promote equality and diversity
2 maintain confidentiality
3 promote individuals' rights and beliefs.

These core principles underpin the work of those providing health, social or early years care. They provide guidelines and ways of working for care settings and their staff. They aim to eliminate discrimination and reduce inequalities by promoting equality and diversity. They also help to ensure individuals' needs are met by the care and support services they use; for example, by maintaining confidentiality and promoting individuals' rights and beliefs.

Table 2.1 **Applying the values of care**

Applying the values of care ensures that service users:	Applying the values of care ensures that practitioners and care workers:
• are treated fairly and with respect • know their rights are maintained • are safe and protected from harm • have their needs met.	• provide effective care • use good practice • provide a consistently high standard of care • prevent discrimination and reduce inequalities • follow legal requirements such as the Equality Act (see LO3, page 52).

Where the values of care are applied

REVISED

The values of care should be applied in all types of health, **social care**, and early years care and education settings. Examples of **care settings** are shown in Figures 2.1, 2.2 and 2.3.

Social care: the provision of personal care, protection or support services for children and adults in need or at risk. Needs may arise from illness, disability, old age or poverty. Social care involves practical support with personal and daily living tasks and emotional support where necessary, as well as providing protection services for children or adults in need or at risk of harm.

Care setting: anywhere that care is provided. Different care settings provide different types of care.

Figure 2.1 **Examples of healthcare settings**

Figure 2.2 Examples of social care settings

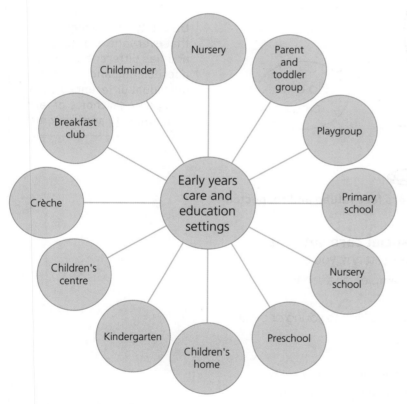

Figure 2.3 Examples of early years care and education settings

Now test yourself

TESTED ☐

1 What is the meaning of the term 'values of care'? [2]
2 Explain why it is important for service users that values of care are applied by care workers. [6]
3 Identify a health setting, a social care setting and an early years setting. [3]

How the values of care are applied in health and social care settings

Remember: the values of care in health and social care are:

1 promoting **equality** and **diversity**
2 maintaining confidentiality
3 promoting individuals' rights and beliefs.

Promoting equality and diversity

This means:

- understanding the basis of discrimination, such as gender, disability, race, age, sexuality or social class
- no discriminatory behaviour, such as prejudice, stereotyping or labelling
- understanding and valuing diversity.

Figure 2.4 It is important that service users feel valued and respected by care workers

Promoting equality in health and social care settings

To promote equality in health and social care settings, you can:

- use non-discriminatory language – for example, call a service user by their name not 'dear' or 'love'
- avoid being patronising; for example, when talking to young or older people
- meet individual needs regarding:
  - mobility: ensure all areas and resources are accessible to all by providing, for example, ramps, automatic doors and adjustable height tables where necessary
  - communication needs: provide 'easy read' versions of information, hearing loops, and information in different formats such as Braille or languages as appropriate; use sign language
  - dietary needs: ensure variety in meals offered, for example, to suit halal, kosher, diabetic, gluten-free and vegetarian diets
  - support cultural needs: provide prayer rooms, transport to church and opportunities to celebrate service users' cultures and religions

Equality: enabling individuals to have the same rights, access and opportunities as everyone else regardless of gender, race, ability, age, sexual orientation or religious belief.

Diversity: the recognition that everyone is different and has different needs, so appreciating and respecting individual differences such as a person's choice of faith, diet, ethnicity and customs.

- treat all individuals fairly irrespective of age, race, gender, religion, disability, ethnicity, sexuality:
  - give all individuals the same choices and opportunities regardless of differences
  - no racist, sexist, ageist comments or actions
  - challenge discrimination
  - arrange visits to places with wheelchair access, hearing loops, and so on.

Promoting diversity in health and social care settings

To promote diversity in health and social care settings, you can do the following.

- Accept and respect individual differences, such as faith, language, diet, customs.
- Provide activities, resources and food that reflect different cultures, beliefs and faiths.
- Celebrate a range of religious and non-religious festivals in the care setting, to reflect the different faiths and cultural needs of the service users.
- Challenge and report any discriminatory behaviour (whether by service users or staff).
- Ensure access to all activities for those less mobile; for example, by providing transport and carers to accompany service users on trips; by visiting wheelchair-accessible venues, and so on.
- Respect service users' cultural and religious requirements; for example:
  - at times it may be appropriate to have a female care assistant, nurse or GP
  - provide prayer rooms and transport to church
  - provide meals in line with these, for example, halal, kosher.
- Support all communication needs so that no one is excluded; for example, provide information in Braille, make hearing loops available, have staff available who can use sign language.

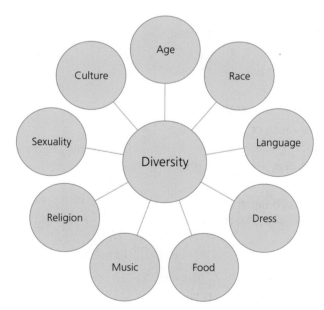

Figure 2.5 Diversity can take many forms

Maintaining confidentiality

This means:

- preventing unauthorised people from accessing personal information
- meeting legal requirements for keeping and using personal information.

Maintaining confidentiality in health and social care settings

- Do not gossip about the service users to their friends and family.
- Share information with other practitioners only on a 'need to know' basis – and only with those directly involved in caring for the individual.
- Keep patient records secure: lock them in a filing cabinet or, if stored electronically, keep them password-protected.
- Keep personal details, files and records safe and secure by not leaving them lying around the care setting for unauthorised people to see.
- Use a private office or empty room for meetings with residents or their family to discuss treatment or care.
- Do not discuss patients, residents or other service users in public places.
- Inform service users of circumstances when information cannot be kept confidential; for example, because the service user is a danger to self or to others, or is at risk of harm.

Promoting individuals' rights and beliefs

This means:

- valuing all individuals
- acting in the best interests of the service user
- freedom from discrimination
- treating individuals with respect and dignity.

Promoting individuals' rights and beliefs in health and social care settings

- Give service users choice; for example, over diet, which clothes to wear, which activities to take part in.
- Maintain privacy – knock on the door before entering a resident's room; pull curtains round a hospital bed.
- Provide access to an advocate for an adult with learning disabilities.
- For those with religious beliefs, provide a prayer room or transport to a church/mosque.
- Provide access to a translator if the service user's first language is not English.
- Always explain any procedures to be carried out as a patient has the right to refuse treatment once they have heard all of the necessary information.

Being a reflective practitioner

The values of care in health and social care are also applied by being a 'reflective practitioner'. To find out what this means, and how to practise it in health and social care settings, turn to page 44.

Now test yourself answers at **www.hoddereducation.co.uk/myrevisionnotes**

Exam tip

Examples can be interchangeable, particularly for rights/beliefs and for equality/diversity – but you will not get credit for repeats in the examination, so make sure you give different examples. Providing a prayer room is an example of a care setting supporting an individual's rights and beliefs. It is also an example of how a care setting can value diversity.

Common mistake

Thinking that equality means to 'treat everyone the same'. This is incorrect: people need to be treated differently according to their needs. For example, some people need, and get, more care, help and attention because of their abilities or a condition or illness.

Revision activity

Learn a range of examples of how practitioners in health and social care settings can apply each of the three values of care.

Now test yourself

TESTED ☐

1 State the three different values of care applied in health and social care settings. [3]
2 Define 'diversity'. [1]
3 What is the meaning of 'equality'? [1]
4 Give **two** examples of how staff at a retirement home could promote diversity. [2]
5 Give **two** examples of how a social worker could promote equality in her day-to-day work at a retirement home. [2]
6 Identify **two** ways confidentiality could be maintained on a hospital ward. [2]
7 Explain **two** ways staff at a residential care setting for young adults with learning disabilities could support users' individual rights and beliefs. [4]

How the early years values of care are applied in settings

Ensuring the welfare of the child is paramount

- The needs of the child should always come first.
- Use a child-centred approach.
- Children must never be humiliated.
- Children must never be abused or smacked.
- Follow safeguarding procedures; for example, all staff must be DBS checked; appoint a designated child protection officer.
- Positive expectations should be encouraged; for example, primary school staff must have a view that all children can succeed and must give appropriate support for their level of ability.

Keeping children safe and maintaining a healthy and safe environment

- Follow health and safety procedures, policies and legislation; for example:
  - have regular fire drills
  - provide safety scissors and equipment
  - ensure regular **PAT testing** of electrical equipment
  - carry out risk assessments of activities, visits and equipment.
- Protect children from abuse; for example, by:
  - ensuring DBS checks for all adults in the setting
  - having child protection procedures in place in the setting.
- Provide meals that meet healthy eating guidelines.
- Have an appropriate adult–child or staff–pupil ratio based on the age of the child and in line with government recommendations.
- Ensure a clean and hygienic environment.
- Train staff in first aid and in the use of an Epipen.

Working in partnership with parents/guardians and families

This can be done through:
- regular parent evenings and meet the mentor sessions
- open days, inviting parents in to see children working
- inviting parents in to discuss progress and/or issues; for example, problem behaviour
- regular progress reports
- reward certificates sent home
- newsletters sent or e-mailed home
- obtaining parents' permission for visits and trips
- phone calls home to discuss any issues
- sharing comments on a child's work
- daily diary provided by a nursery

Figure 2.6 The early years values of care

Exam tip

You need to be able to give examples of how care workers would apply each of the values of care in their day-to-day work in an early years setting.

PAT testing: Portable Appliance Testing is the term used to describe the checking of electrical appliances and equipment to ensure they are safe to use.

- informing parents about accidents or incidents
- informal chats with parents; for example, on arrival to drop off or collect children
- providing information sessions and training for parents on relevant topics; for example, potty training, dealing with tantrums, how to help your child learn to read, all about the nursery curriculum and so on.

Encouraging children's learning and development

Children should be offered a range of experiences to enhance learning.

- Provide a range of activities and have a well planned curriculum.
- Offer differentiated worksheets and activities to cater for all abilities.
- Design activities to stretch learning.
- Monitor children's progress.
- Introduce additional activities to stretch and challenge.
- Offer activities suited to children's developmental progress.
- Make activities stimulating and engaging to encourage children's learning.

Valuing diversity

- Teach about various traditions, customs and festivals to raise awareness of different cultures
- Resources such as DVDs and toys should reflect different cultures and beliefs.
- Posters and displays should present positive role models from different cultures.
- Celebrate a wide range of festivals with all of the children; for example, Diwali, Christmas, Chinese New Year, and so on, to raise awareness of diversity.
- Have school 'welcome' signs in different languages.
- Provide books in different languages.
- Invite guest speakers to talk about different cultures.
- Offer food options to suit different diets, such as vegetarian, gluten free, halal, kosher.
- Challenge discrimination as it occurs; for example, if a child or staff member makes racist or sexist comments.
- Differentiate tasks and activities to meet children's individual needs.
- Allow time off school for festivals that relate to children's religious beliefs, for example, Eid.

Figure 2.7 Valuing diversity: a school 'welcome' sign showing 'Hello' in 13 languages

Ensuring equality of opportunity

- Provide each child with the opportunity to work towards his/her potential.
- Ensure all areas of the setting are accessible to all and make adaptations if needed; for example, by providing ramps, wider doorways, adjustable height tables.
- Ensure all resources – worksheets, books, outside play and so on – are available to all children.
- Ensure activities are accessible for all children to participate in, regardless of gender or disabilities.
- Work to meet children's individual needs, whether cultural, religious, mobility, dietary or communication.
- Use non-discriminatory language.
- All children should be treated fairly and staff should have no favourites.
- Make sure staff are familiar with, and follow, the setting's equal opportunities policy.

Practising anti-discrimination

- Do not discriminate on the basis of gender, social background, race or anything else.
- Challenge any discriminatory comments or actions by children or staff.
- Ensure no one is excluded from activities; for example, by providing sign language, a hearing loop or wheelchair access if needed.
- Challenge stereotypical views, such as 'boys will be boys', 'girls are little princesses', and so on.
- Be a good role model by demonstrating inclusive behaviour.

> **Common mistake**
>
> **Having 'girls' toys' and 'boys' toys' promotes equality.** To promote equality it is best to provide 'gender neutral' toys that can be played with by both boys and girls, such as Lego.

Figure 2.8 Activities should be accessible for all children

Ensuring confidentiality

- Share information with other practitioners on a 'need-to-know' basis only.
- Keep children's personal information secure; for example, in a locked filing cabinet or password protected if electronic.
- Never gossip about the child's family circumstances.
- Never discuss children in public places.
- Ensure meetings with parents are private, i.e., behind closed doors.

Working with others (to include other professionals or in partnership)

- Work with other agencies/practitioners/services that support children, such as:
  - school nurse
  - social worker
  - health visitor
  - GP
  - police.
- Information should be shared openly but sensitively between practitioners directly involved in caring for the child.

How the early years values of care are applied in settings

Exam tip

In the examination, if you are asked to identify the values for health and social care, you must always **use the exact wording** or you will not get the mark. For example:
- 'anti-discrimination' should be *'practising* anti-discrimination'
- 'working with families' should be 'working *in partnership with parents/guardians and* families'
- 'keeping children safe' should be 'keeping children safe *and maintaining a healthy and safe environment'*.

Revision activity

Create a set of revision cards for the early years values of care. On each card:
- write down the name of the value of care
- give examples showing how it could be applied in early years care settings.

Now test yourself
TESTED ☐

1 Give an example of how a nursery assistant could apply each of the following early years values of care in their day-to-day work.
   (a) working in partnership with parents/guardians and families
   (b) ensuring confidentiality
   (c) ensuring the welfare of the child is paramount. [3]
2 Give **two** examples of other professionals a primary school teacher might work with and suggest a reason for each. [4]
3 Explain ways a care setting could avoid discriminating against children with a disability. [8]
4 Explain **three** ways early years workers in a nursery could ensure children are kept safe. [3]

The importance of applying the values of care in early years care settings

Applying the values of care means:

- all children receive appropriate care and attention
- all children feel safe
- children feel valued
- children are kept safe
- individual needs are met
- children are treated fairly
- children are given opportunities to support their development
- special needs are provided for
- good relationships are promoted
- trust can be established
- children have increased self-esteem and self-confidence
- children are respected
- children's rights are promoted
- legislation (laws) are followed
- staff who value diversity act as role models – by setting an example, this teaches children not to discriminate
- children don't feel stupid or patronised.

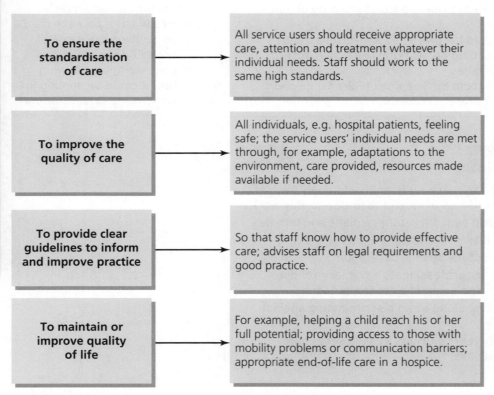

To ensure the standardisation of care	All service users should receive appropriate care, attention and treatment whatever their individual needs. Staff should work to the same high standards.
To improve the quality of care	All individuals, e.g. hospital patients, feeling safe; the service users' individual needs are met through, for example, adaptations to the environment, care provided, resources made available if needed.
To provide clear guidelines to inform and improve practice	So that staff know how to provide effective care; advises staff on legal requirements and good practice.
To maintain or improve quality of life	For example, helping a child reach his or her full potential; providing access to those with mobility problems or communication barriers; appropriate end-of-life care in a hospice.

Figure 2.9 Why it is important for care workers to apply the values of care

Figure 2.10 The importance of applying the values of care

The values of care have a big impact on the care provided in health, social care and early years settings as they help to ensure the following.

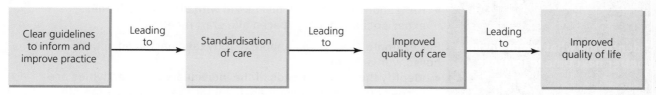

Figure 2.11 The impact of applying the values of care in health, social care and early years settings

Revision activity

Choose ten points from the bullet list above and, for each point, explain a specific action that a care worker could take to achieve it.

Exam tip

Read the examination question carefully. Is it asking about applying values of care in a health and social care setting or in an early years setting; or is it asking for general points that could apply to both settings?

Empowerment: the process that enables individuals to take control of their lives and make their own decisions. Giving someone confidence in their own abilities.

Now test yourself   TESTED ☐

1 Explain **four** main reasons why it is important to apply the values of care. [8]
2 Give the meaning of the term 'empowerment'. [1]
3 Give **four** ways in which applying the values of care can empower individuals. [4]

Reflective practice

All care practitioners, in whatever type of setting, will apply the values of care by being a **reflective practitioner**.

There are four main aspects to being a reflective practitioner:

- exploring your training and development needs
- evaluating specific incidents or activities
- identifying what might be done better next time to improve
- identifying what went well.

> **Reflective practitioner**: someone who regularly looks back at the work they do, and how they do it, to consider how they can improve their practice.

Table 2.2 Examples of reflective practice for an early years care worker

Exploring training and development needs	• The care worker critically evaluates their own performance. • Training needs are identified to improve their knowledge, skills and understanding. For example, training in the values of care, 'phonics', first aid, safeguarding procedures, and so on.
Evaluating specific incidents or activities	• The care worker investigates a breach of confidentiality or an accident in the early years setting. Questions to ask: ○ When, why, how, did it happen? ○ How can it be avoided next time? • The appropriateness of set tasks and activities is evaluated against children's progress. • Reflections are shared: discussed with other practitioners; experiences/learning shared at a staff meeting.
Identifying what might be done better next time to improve	For example, if a child is unable to fully take part in an activity or gets bored with an activity: • Identify the specific needs of the individual so that activities are accessible, engaging and beneficial for the child; for example, adaptation of premises (hearing loop, wheelchair access) or activities adapted to stretch and challenge, and better engage, child.
Identifying what went well	• What were the children doing? • What were they learning? • Was it worthwhile? • What should they do next?

Revision activity

Learn the four main aspects of reflective practice.

Exam tip

Remember to use your knowledge from different parts of the specification, such as applying values of care, rights and effective communication, to answer questions about reflective practice.

Table 2.3 Examples of reflective practice for care workers in a GP surgery

Issue	Reflective practice	Care workers will	Examples of impact on daily practice
Patients complain there is no privacy	Evaluating specific incidents or activities	Identify situations when patients may be overheard when talking about personal information	Care workers use a private room/area, when required, to maintain patients' privacy and confidentiality
Staff are impolite; they show lack of respect and patients feel patronised	Exploring training and development needs	Review own knowledge and practice and undertake training to improve knowledge and understanding about effective communication with patients	Patients treated with respect through: • care workers listening to them/use of active listening skills • adapting communication to meet the needs of the individual • patients not talked down to/patronised.
Lack of access to the GP surgery for patients in wheelchairs	Identifying what might be done better	Identify specific needs of individuals to ensure access for all	Adaptation of premises, such as ramps, automatic doors, wider doorways

Common mistake

Defining 'reflective practice' as 'a practitioner who reflects on their own practice'. Never use the words you are defining in the definition, as you will just be repeating what you are supposed to be defining. It is better to say something like: 'Someone who regularly looks back at the work they do, and how they do it, to consider how they can improve their practice.'

Now test yourself

TESTED ☐

1 What is the meaning of the term 'reflective practice'? [1]
2 State the **four** key aspects of reflective practice. [4]
3 A child has injured themselves during a cut and stick activity that you organised. Use the four aspects of reflective practice as headings and carry out a reflection on what happened. State what could be done better next time. [5]

The effects on people who use services if the values of care are not applied

Examples of values of care not being applied

- Incidents of inappropriate breaking of confidentiality; for example, an individual's personal records left lying around.
- Staff gossiping about the children.
- Equipment and toys not safety checked, not repaired, not PAT tested.
- Failure to carry out risk assessments.
- No provision for special diets.
- No provision for different cultures.
- No provision for disabilities, such as learning, mobility.
- No safeguarding procedures.
- No policies on, for example, health and safety, equal opportunities, bullying.
- No planning of activities.
- Lack of communication with parents or other professionals.
- Failure to challenge incidents of discrimination.

The effects on individuals of these failures to apply the values of care can be:

- physical
- intellectual
- emotional
- social.

> **Exam tip**
>
> It can help to remember the effects of the values of care not being applied as the 'PIES' (Physical, Intellectual, Emotional, Social) effects.

Physical effects

The physical effects if the values of care are not applied relate to an individual's body. Not applying the values of care may lead to poor physical health and well-being.

Some examples of possible physical effects are:

- dehydration; for example, if a person doesn't like drinking tea or other drinks they are given without consultation
- malnutrition and/or eating disorders; for example, if an individual stops eating meals due to boredom or dislike of what is provided, or if inappropriate food is provided, such as no vegetarian options or no gluten-free food for individuals with coeliac disease
- self-harm due to depression, lack of stimulation or social interaction, or mental health issues
- the individual's general health could deteriorate due to poor care; for example, they could become unfit and gain weight because they are not provided with opportunities to exercise; or they lack energy for exercise due to a poor diet
- injuries such as cuts, grazes and bruises or even broken bones, as the result of abusive treatment or poor manual handling by untrained care workers, or due to trip hazards and old equipment in need of repair
- an existing illness could get worse without proper treatment or if medications are not provided at the correct times.

Now test yourself answers at www.hoddereducation.co.uk/myrevisionnotes

Intellectual effects

Intellectual means an individual's thought processes, such as thinking skills, understanding, learning, reasoning, comprehension and knowledge.

Some examples of possible intellectual effects if the values of care are not applied are as follows.

- For a child with learning difficulties who is not given support and learning activities matched to their special needs:
  - lack of skills development, such as poor skills in writing, reading, and so on
  - limited ability to communicate, limited vocabulary
  - lack of knowledge
  - lack of progress, leading to restricted study and employment opportunities in later life
  - lack of achievement
  - failure to achieve potential; for example, may not get a challenging and rewarding job in the future.
- For a care home resident left in front of the television every day or a child not being engaged, encouraged and stretched by lessons:
  - lack of mental stimulation
  - loss of focus/concentration
  - lack of interest.

> **Exam tip**
>
> It is important to realise that effects do not occur in isolation but are interrelated (they affect one another). For example, a practitioner being bullied at work may suffer physical harm such as bruises. This could lead them to feel unsafe, causing them to take time off work so as to avoid the bully. Not going to work could lead to lack of career progress or them losing their job.

Emotional effects

Emotional effects relate to an individual's feelings. If hospital patients are not consulted regarding their care, or if staff are too busy to answer their questions or explain treatments and medication, over time the emotional impacts can be significant. A primary school child who is never praised for their work, or who is not helped when they are bullied, can suffer long lasting and severe emotional distress.

Some examples of possible emotional effects if the values of care are not applied as follows.

Feeling disempowered

- Individuals feel unwanted and unimportant.
- They may feel a lack of control over their life.
- Individuals become disengaged with life and lose interest.
- An individual may feel demoralised and not motivated to achieve.
- The individual may start to think that carers know best.
- An individual may accept whatever happens, and no longer be bothered to complain.
- It may lead to behaviour changes; for example, they may become aggressive or unco-operative.
- This may lead to loss of independence; for example, feeling they can't make decisions.
- An individual can be left feeling betrayed; for example, if confidentiality was broken.

Loss of self-confidence

- A lack of support restricts opportunities available to individuals, which prevents them from gaining self-confidence/does not help to empower them.
- An individual could develop low self-esteem and feel they are not capable of achieving anything.
- They may feel frustrated because they are not allowed to do anything for themselves.
- It can result in **learned helplessness** and loss of motivation.
- An individual may be scared to tell carers what they want or need.

> **Disempowerment**: feeling that you have a lack of control over your life and lack independence.
>
> **Learned helplessness**: when someone gives up trying as a result of consistent lack of achievement or reward – they come to believe that it is not worth trying because they will fail anyway.

Table 2.4 Emotional effects on individuals if the values of care are not applied

Emotional effects	Possible impacts
- angry/annoyed/frustrated - devalued - embarrassed - feeling scared/frightened - feeling inadequate - humiliation - loss of trust - low self-confidence - low self-esteem - feeling unsafe - stress - unhappy/upset - feelings of worthlessness	- becomes withdrawn and does not want to join in with others - does not want to attend the care setting, such as school - develops behaviour problems - becomes aggressive towards others, loss of trust - increased risk of injuries, accidents - loss of concentration, leading to lack of progress and underachievement - failure to thrive, developmental delay

Now test yourself answers at **www.hoddereducation.co.uk/myrevisionnotes**

Social effects

The social effects on people if the values of care are not applied relate to an individual's relationship with others. For example, a care home resident could become isolated and lonely if carers do not seem interested in her and just talk among themselves rather than engaging with her.

Some examples of possible social effects if the values of care are not applied are:

- living alone, being socially isolated, feeling lonely
- becoming anti-social/social withdrawal
- behaviour problems
- social exclusion/feeling left out
- poor social skills/less sociable/not wanting to interact with/talk to others
- inability to make relationships
- lack of friends
- feeling **marginalised**
- being unco-operative
- refusing to go to the service/go out at all.

> **Marginalised**: excluded from participating; feeling unimportant and not wanted by the majority of people.

> **Exam tip**
>
> When an examination question asks you to 'explain effects', you need to write about physical, intellectual, emotional and social effects. Make sure you give examples for all four types of effects or you will not gain high marks.

> **Exam tip**
>
> If an examination question asks about emotional and social effects, for example, make sure your answer covers both so that you can get the highest marks. You will only gain a maximum of half marks if you only write about emotional OR social effects.

> **Common mistake**
>
> **Being too vague if an examination question on effects requires a one-word answer**. It is okay to answer with one word, but remember to be precise. For example, stating 'hurt' as an emotional effect is too vague – it could mean physically or emotionally hurt; a better answer would be 'upset' or 'unhappy'.

> **Revision activity**
>
> Learn at least four effects for each of the PIES.

Now test yourself

TESTED ☐

1 What are the meanings of the terms 'physical', 'intellectual', 'emotional' and 'social'? [4]
2 State **two** physical effects and **two** emotional effects on a hospital patient who is not given regular drinks and so does not get enough fluids. [4]
3 Describe the emotional effects on a pregnant woman who is told, without any explanation, that she cannot have a home birth. [2]
4 Jayson is being bullied at primary school. Explain the possible effects on him of being bullied. [6]

LO3: Understand how legislation impacts on care settings

The key aspects of legislation and the groups to which they are relevant

What is legislation?

Legislation:

- is a collection of laws passed by Parliament
- states the rights and entitlements of individuals
- states the responsibilities of individuals and organisations
- is upheld through the courts.

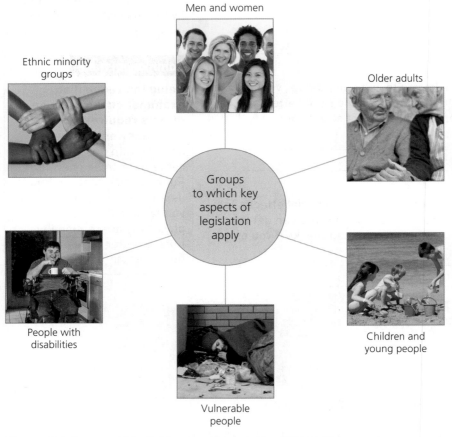

Figure 3.1 Groups of individuals protected by legislation

Although anyone in society can be discriminated against, some groups can be particularly **vulnerable** to discrimination and poor standards of care. These are shown in Figure 3.1.

- Children may not be aware of their rights, so are more at risk of abuse.
- Older people can also be vulnerable; for example, a person with dementia may forget how they have been treated so their abuse is never reported.
- Some people have a **disability**, illness or condition that affects their ability to stand up for their rights or to complain about poor treatment.

Vulnerable: describes an individual who is unable to protect themselves against significant harm or exploitation. This may be because of mental or physical disability or illness.

Disability: a physical or mental impairment that limits a person's movement, senses or activities.

They may be discriminated against; for example, by failure to provide ramps or information in Braille.

- Some people experience discrimination or poor treatment due to their age; for example, by being considered too young or too old to understand important information about their care.
- Men and women may be discriminated against (fail to receive equal opportunities and treatment) due to their gender or sexuality. For example, a man may be promoted over a woman because he is less likely to take extended paternity leave.
- Ethnic minority groups may experience racism (discrimination based on their race or ethnicity); for example, by not being given information in their home languages.

How does legislation support individual rights?

- It sets out the standards of practice and conduct that those who work in the health, social care and early years sectors must meet.
- It provides a legal framework for care that care providers have to comply with.
- It provides a system of **redress**.
- It provides individuals with the right to access and receive care and support.
- It creates regulatory arrangements for the **monitoring** of care standards.

How key legislation impacts

Figure 3.2 The impacts of key legislation

Exam tip

You will need to know the key aspects of these five pieces of legislation (you do not need to know the dates):
- Equality Act 2010
- Children Act 2004
- Data Protection Act 1998
- Health and Safety at Work Act 1974
- Mental Health Act 2007.

Revision activity

Name the six different groups protected by legislation. Explain why each group may need the protection provided by legislation to support their rights.

Common mistake

Naming a piece of legislation without including the word 'Act' at the end. If you do this, you will not get a mark. In your exam you must refer to the Equality Act, the Children Act, the Data Protection Act, the Health and Safety at Work Act and the Mental Health Act.

Now test yourself   TESTED ☐

1 An 85-year-old man requests a different social worker because he thinks his current one is 'too young to know what she is doing'. What type of discrimination is this and why? [2]
2 (a) Identify **four** groups of people in society who are protected by legislation. [4]
  (b) For each group you identified in part (a), explain why they may need protection and support. [4]
3 State how legislation impacts on:
  (a) service users
  (b) service providers
  (c) care practitioners. [3]

An overview of the key aspects of legislation

Equality Act 2010

- Aims to prevent discrimination based on nine 'protected characteristics' (see Figure 3.3). It is unlawful to discriminate on the basis of a protected characteristic.
- Provides protection for people discriminated against because they are associated with someone who has a protected characteristic (so there is now also protection for carers of an individual who has a protected characteristic).
- Makes discrimination in education, employment, access to goods and services and housing illegal.
- Gives women the right to breastfeed in public places.
- Makes pay secrecy clauses illegal (so you cannot be legally prevented from disclosing your income to another).

> **Exam tip**
>
> Make sure you learn the 'key aspects' and 'nine protected characteristics' of the Equality Act, so that you can use the correct terminology when answering exam questions.

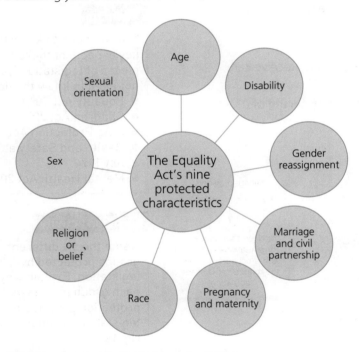

Figure 3.3 The nine protected characteristics

The Equality Act sets out the different ways in which it is unlawful to treat someone, such as:

- **direct** and **indirect discrimination**
- **harassment**
- **victimisation**
- failing to make a reasonable adjustment for a disabled person.

Now consider these examples. How does the Equality Act help to protect individuals from discrimination in these cases?

Example 1: Direct discrimination by a care setting based on a protected characteristic

A woman is told she did not get the job as a Practice Manager because 'she might get pregnant and go on maternity leave' and 'the setting wants continuity and doesn't want someone who might take time off'.

> **Direct discrimination**: intentionally putting someone at a disadvantage or treating them unfairly based on their differences, i.e., their 'protected characteristics'.
>
> **Indirect discrimination**: when a policy, practice or rule applies to everybody but has a detrimental effect on some people. For example, a job advert that states male applicants must be clean-shaven would discriminate against individuals who grow facial hair because of their religious beliefs.
>
> **Harassment**: unwanted behaviour that intends to intimidate or humiliate someone.
>
> **Victimisation**: bad treatment directed towards someone who has made a complaint or has taken action under the Equality Act or similar legislation.
>
> **Gender reassignment**: when a person's physical sexual characteristics are changed by medical procedures such as surgery or hormone treatment.
>
> **Sexual orientation**: an individual's sexual preferences; for example, homosexual or heterosexual.

This is discrimination on the basis of the protected characteristic 'sex', as the care setting does not want a female practice manager of child-bearing age. Staff selection and interview procedures must always comply with the Equality Act so that staff are selected on the basis of the skills they can offer.

Example 2: How care settings can prevent discrimination against a protected characteristic

A wheelchair user is unable to visit his grandmother upstairs in the care home because there are no lifts in the building.

Disability is one of the protected characteristics and so disability discrimination is illegal. Service providers must therefore ensure settings are accessible for **all** staff, service users and visitors, including those with a range of different disabilities; for example, by:

- adapting premises to enable access for wheelchair users, for example, by including ramps and automatic doors
- providing leaflets/information in Braille and large print
- installing **hearing loops**/have staff who know **BSL**
- producing easy-to-understand information for those with learning disabilities
- having an equal opportunities policy
- monitoring the selection and recruitment of staff to see how many individuals with a disability apply for jobs and how many are actually given a job.

> **Hearing loop:** a special type of sound system for use by people with hearing aids. It provides a wireless signal that is picked up by the hearing aid and can greatly improve the quality of sound.
>
> **BSL:** British Sign Language. A communication system of hand movements, gestures, body language and facial expressions used by those who are deaf or have a hearing impairment. Can also be used by non-deaf people to assist with effective communication.

Revision activity

Create a concept map of facts about the Equality Act.

Common mistake

Only giving part of a protected characteristic when asked to name them. For example, stating 'marriage' instead of 'marriage and civil partnership' or 'gender' instead of 'gender reassignment'. You must state the full characteristic or you will not gain the mark.

Now test yourself

TESTED

1 What is the meaning of the term 'protected characteristic'? [1]
2 State **four** key aspects of the Equality Act. [4]
3 Identify **two** ways the Equality Act protects the rights of women. [2]
4 Explain ways a care setting could avoid discriminating against individuals with a disability. [8]

Children Act 2004

Key aspects of the Children Act 2004

- Aims to protect all children at risk of harm and keep them safe.
- Contains the **paramountcy principle**.
- Children have the right to be consulted.
- Children have the right to have an advocate.
- Every Child Matters (ECM).
- Encourages partnership working.
- Created the role of Children's Commissioner.
- Created the legal requirement for Children's Safeguarding Boards.
- Established the Children and Young People's Plan (CYPP).

> **Paramountcy principle:** the child's best interest and welfare is the first and most important consideration.

Table 3.1 Impact of the Children Act 2004 on service providers, practitioners and children

Key aspects of Children Act 2004	Impact on practitioners/service providers/children
Aims to protect all children at risk of harm and keep them safe	May involve practitioners in taking a child away from family, through the use of care orders or emergency protection orders. It is the duty of practitioners who work with children to follow safeguarding procedures.
Paramountcy principle	Issues have to be determined as soon as possible and children's needs must come first; so taking a child away from their family may adversely affect the adults involved but may be in the child's best interests.
Children have the right to be consulted	Children who are mature and old enough are consulted. This gives children the right to speak out and have their opinions listened to and taken into account when decisions are made. Examples include if their parents were divorcing they would be consulted by the court about which parent they want to live with; or if they were being taken into care due to neglect they would be consulted about other members of the wider family they could live with.
Children have the right to have an advocate	Children have a right to an advocate to represent them. Children have to be consulted and their wishes taken into consideration. Practitioners have to ensure children stay within the wider family circle where possible rather than being placed in care.
Every Child Matters – five outcomes (ECM)	The five outcomes of Every Child Matters (ECM) are aims for every child: staying safe, being healthy, enjoying and achieving, making a positive contribution and economic well-being. ECM puts a duty on local authorities to promote co-operation between agencies/practitioners to improve the well-being of children and young people relating to the five outcomes.
Encourages partnership working	Care practitioners who work with children must follow safeguarding procedures. To protect children they also have a duty to ensure information is shared with appropriate teams, such as social care, health and early years, who are also involved in caring for a child.
Created role of Children's Commissioner. Set up local Children's Safeguarding Boards. Established Children and Young People's Plan (CYPP)	These all give children a voice and represent their interests locally and nationally. The role of the Children's Commissioner is to raise awareness of the best interests of children and to report annually to Parliament.

Revision activity

To help you remember the five outcomes of Every Child Matters (ECM), use the acronym: **SHEEP:**
- **S**taying safe
- **H**ealthy (being)
- **E**njoying and achieving
- **E**conomic well-being
- **P**ositive contribution (making a)

Figure 3.4 Use the acronym 'SHEEP' to help you remember the five outcomes of ECM

Exam tip

Learn the key aspects of the Children Act. This will enable you to give specific examples of what the Act covers and you will also be able to use the correct terminology when answering the questions.

Common mistake

Calling the Act the 'Children's Act'. This is incorrect and will not gain a mark in an exam question. The correct name of the Act is the Children Act.

Revision activity

For each of the key aspects of the Children Act, write a sentence about the impact it has on a care practitioner's work.

Now test yourself

TESTED ☐

1 (a) Identify **four** key aspects of the Children Act 2004. [4]
   (b) Give **one** impact on practitioners for each key aspect you gave in part (a). [4]
2 (a) What does ECM stand for? [1]
   (b) List the **five** outcomes of ECM. [5]
3 Explain how the Children Act supports children's rights. [6]

Data Protection Act 1998

The Data Protection Act has eight key principles that state how data (information) should be kept and handled:

Data and information should be

- processed fairly and lawfully
- used only for the purposes for which it was intended
- adequate and relevant but not excessive
- accurate and kept up-to-date
- kept for no longer than is necessary
- processed in line with the rights of the individual
- secured
- kept in the UK and not transferred to other countries outside the European economic area (the EU).

Table 3.2 The impact of the Data Protection Act principles on service providers and practitioners

Key principles *Data and information should be*	Impact on service providers, practitioners and service users
Processed fairly and lawfully	Care service providers should not collect and use personal information without the permission of the individual using the care service. Personal information should only be used on a 'need-to-know' basis.
Used only for the purposes for which it was intended	Care settings should only hold service users' information for a clear purpose and must only use it for that purpose.
Adequate and relevant but not excessive	Practitioners in care settings should only collect and use information that is needed; they should not collect unnecessary information. For example, a fully detailed case history would not be required by a nurse at A&E treating a teenager with a sprained ankle, but it would be required by a social worker to inform care planning for an older adult who lives alone.
Accurate and kept up-to-date	Inaccurate/incorrect data should be destroyed or corrected. Staff have a responsibility to ensure information is correct. Systems should be in place for checking accuracy, for instance, asking patients/residents/parents.
Kept for no longer than is necessary	Information should be deleted or destroyed by the service provider or practitioner when it is no longer needed – by securely deleting or shredding sensitive or personal data. For example, the personnel records of a practitioner who no longer works in a care setting or the personal records of a care home resident who has left the care home should be destroyed.
Processed in line with the rights of the individual	People have a right to: • know what information is being held about them by care services • know how their information is being used • have any errors corrected • prevent any data being used for advertising or marketing.
Secured	Non-authorised staff/people should not be allowed to access the information, which should be kept in secure conditions; there should be clear guidelines on who can have access.
Not transferred to countries outside the European economic area	Information should not be transferred outside the EU (the European economic area), unless the service user has given consent. This is because other countries may not have the same data protection legislation and so data may not be secure.

Now test yourself answers at **www.hoddereducation.co.uk/myrevisionnotes**

Now test yourself

TESTED

1 Identify **four** principles of the Data Protection Act 1998. [4]
2 Describe **two** ways that care setting staff could follow the requirements of the Data Protection Act. [4]
3 Read **A–E** below. Which are examples of maintaining confidentiality and which are examples of the Data Protection Act principles?
   A Data should be kept for no longer than is necessary.
   B A nurse arranges a meeting with a patient in a private room to update the patient's medical records.
   C Children's progress records are kept in a locked filing cabinet.
   D Service users' records are kept on a password-protected computer.
   E Information must be secured against accidental loss, damage or unlawful processing. [5]
4 Discuss how the Data Protection Act 1998 supports the rights of individuals to confidentiality. [6]

Health and Safety at Work Act 1974

Table 3.3 Requirements of HASAWA for service providers

Key aspects of the Act	Requires that employers:
• The working environment must not put anyone at risk	• Must carry out risk assessments. • Must provide **PPE**. • Put in place procedures to prevent accidents. • Monitor staff practice. • Have working fire alarms, extinguishers and accessible fire doors.
• The equipment provided must be safe and in good working order	• Provide equipment that is fit for purpose and in good working order. • Carry out regular safety checks of all equipment. • Regularly service/maintain all equipment. • PAT test electrical appliances.
• Employers must provide adequate health and safety training for staff	• Provide health and safety training for staff, which is updated regularly. • Train staff in the use of specialist equipment. • Hold regular fire/evacuation practices. • Provide adequate first aid.
• A written health and safety policy should be provided	• Produce a health and safety policy in line with legal requirements. • Ensure staff are aware of, and have access to, the policy. • Display the 'Health and Safety Law' poster in the workplace.
• Protective equipment, if needed, must be available free of charge to **employees**	• Maintain an adequate supply of PPE. • Make no charge to staff for PPE. • Ensure staff wear the PPE provided.

Table 3.4 Requirements of HASAWA for employees

Key aspects of the Act	Requires that employees:
• The working environment must not put anyone at risk	• Must report any hazards to the employer. • Must take care of themselves and others in the workplace.
• The equipment provided must be safe and in good working order	• Must not misuse or tamper with equipment provided that meets health and safety regulations, e.g. fire extinguishers.
• Employers must provide adequate health and safety training for staff	• Must co-operate with their employer by attending health and safety training.
• A written health and safety policy should be provided	• Must co-operate with their employer by following health and safety regulations in the workplace.
• Protective equipment, if needed, must be available free of charge to employees	• Must wear any protective clothing provided

> **Exam tip**
>
> Always write 'Health and Safety at Work Act' out in full if you are asked to name the legislation. However, to save time when writing an extended answer, you can refer to the Act using the abbreviation HASAWA.

> **PPE**: personal protective equipment provided by your employer. This is any clothing and protective equipment designed to ensure personal safety in the workplace.
>
> **Employees**: practitioners, care workers and other staff in a care setting.

> **Exam tip**
>
> Always read the examination question carefully. If there is a question on the Health and Safety at Work Act, check: is the question asking about employers' responsibilities or employees' responsibilities, or both?

How does the Health and Safety at Work Act support individuals' rights?

- Ensures a safe working environment.
- Risk assessments must be carried out to prevent accidents.
- All settings must have a health and safety policy that meets legal requirements.
- Protective equipment and clothing to be provided when needed.
- All staff to have health and safety training.
- All settings to have emergency procedures, such as fire drills.
- Equipment must be fit for purpose and staff trained in how to use it.

Exam tip

Learn the key aspects of the Health and Safety at Work Act that apply to employers as well as employees. This will enable you to give detailed answers with examples for extended writing questions.

Revision activity

Produce two spider diagrams: one for the employer's health and safety responsibilities under HASAWA and one for the employee's responsibilities.

Common mistake

Not being specific in answers. Be clear about whether you are writing about the service provider's health and safety responsibilities or the care worker's responsibilities.

Now test yourself

TESTED ☐

1 What does the abbreviation PPE stand for? [2]
2 Give **two** examples of PPE that a care worker might need. [2]
3 List **three** ways a service provider could ensure that the equipment provided is safe and in good working order. [3]
4 Explain a care worker's responsibilities to ensure safety of self and others in the workplace. [6]

Mental Health Act 2007

Key aspects of the Mental Health Act 2007

- Aims to protect those at risk to themselves or others.
- Provides the legal authority for an individual to be taken to a 'place of safety' for assessment.
- Provides a definition of mental disorder.
- Gives rights to those with a mental disorder.
- Sets out safeguards (protective measures) to which the person with a mental disorder is entitled.
- Established Managers' Hearings and Mental Health Review Tribunals to review decisions regarding individuals' care.

Sectioning

The Mental Health Act states that an individual can be taken to hospital and treated against their wishes. This is known as being 'sectioned'. Sectioning can only happen when:

- you have a mental disorder that puts you or others at risk of harm
- three specially trained professionals agree that the person's mental health puts themselves or others at risk of harm and the individual needs to be in hospital for assesment and treatment.

When someone is sectioned:

- they can be given treatment even if they do not want it
- they have the right to appeal against it and the right to get help from an advocate.

An individual can only be sectioned if they have a serious mental disorder. The Mental Health Act defines the term 'mental disorder' as 'any disorder or disability of the mind'. It includes mental health conditions such as: schizophrenia, severe depression, bipolar disorder, anxiety disorder, obsessive-compulsive disorder, eating disorders and personality disorders.

Figure 3.5 Sectioning can only happen when you have a mental disorder that puts you or others at risk of harm

Now test yourself answers at www.hoddereducation.co.uk/myrevisionnotes

Table 3.5 The impact of the Mental Health Act on service providers and practitioners

Aspects of the Mental Health Act	Impact on service providers and practitioners
Aims to protect those at risk to themselves or others **Provides the authority to take the person to a 'place of safety' for assessment** **Sets out the processes that must be followed to detain a person with a mental disorder** **An 'appropriate medical treatment test' is required for a longer detention**	• Need to be able to make difficult decisions, such as taking the person to a place of safety without their consent (sectioning). • Practitioners must be appropriately qualified – an 'approved social worker' and a 'responsible medical officer' are needed to make the decision to section. • Duty of care – practitioners must follow procedures that safeguard those with a mental disorder/ensure information is shared. • Personal skills and qualities – must be able to communicate well with those who have a mental disorder and their families. • Practitioners can only detain the person for initial assessment for up to 28 days. • Practitioners have the duty to provide the person with an independent mental health advocate. • Practitioners have to provide appropriate '**supervised community treatment**' following release from hospital. • It is the duty of practitioners who work with those who have a mental disorder to follow the correct procedures. • Practitioners must ensure appropriate medical treatment is available to continue the detention of the person beyond 28 days.

Table 3.6 The impact of the Mental Health Act on service users

Aspects of the Mental Health Act	Impact on service user's
Aims to keep people safe **Gives rights to those with a mental disorder** **Sets out safeguards to which the person with a mental disorder is entitled** **Provides a definition of mental disorder** **Established Managers' Hearings and Mental Health Review Tribunals**	• Practitioners follow set procedures that safeguard those with a mental disorder and ensure information is shared for the service user's safety. • Service users have the right to an independent mental health advocate. • Service users have the right to appropriate supervised community treatment following release from hospital. • Practitioners must represent the best interests of those with a mental health disorder. • To ensure accountability of those who make decisions, checks are made by independent bodies.

Supervised community treatment: individuals can be treated in the community for their mental health problem instead of staying in hospital, but with conditions attached, such as they may have to live in a certain place and attend appointments for treatment. They can be returned to hospital for immediate treatment if necessary.

How does the Mental Health Act support individuals' rights?

- Protects people who lose the ability to make decisions for themselves.
- Prevents an individual from harming themselves or others by allowing a compulsory section order.
- Clearly defines what constitutes a mental disorder.
- The individual has a right to have an advocate.
- Very careful procedures have to be followed when admitting the person against their will to make sure their rights are safeguarded.
- Systems are in place (Review Tribunals and Managers' Hearings) to ensure accountability of those making the decision to 'section' the individual.
- This legislation does not apply to everyone with a mental disorder – only those whose condition is likely to pose a threat to themselves or others.

Exam tip

Learn at least four of the key aspects of the Mental Health Act – two where you can explain the impact on service providers and two where you can explain the impact on service users.

Revision activity

Read the 'Mental Health Act Factsheet' available from the mental health charity Rethink (www.rethink.org).

Common mistake

Not being able to state specific key aspects of the Mental Health Act. Make sure that you learn at least four aspects so that you know the correct terminology to use in your answers.

Now test yourself

TESTED

1 Explain the meaning of the term 'sectioning'. [3]
2 State **two** key aspects of the Mental Health Act and explain how each impacts on practitioners. [4]
3 Describe **two** ways the Mental Health Act supports individual rights. [4]

How key legislation impacts on people who use services, care practitioners and service providers

REVISED

Table 3.7 The impact of legislation on people who use services, care practitioners and service providers

People who use services	• will know the rights to which they are entitled • can exercise their rights, such as to choice, to consultation, when using care and support services • have a system of redress through the courts • are protected, e.g. protection provided under the Equality Act and the Children Act.
Care practitioners	• will need training on the requirements of legislation • the legislation sets the standards of practice and conduct that are required • must follow guidance, for example, on data protection • will be aware of their responsibilities.
Service providers	• will know what is required to operate within the law • have a framework to help them maintain and improve the quality of service • have to produce organisational policies and procedures • must make reasonable adjustments to ensure the setting is accessible.

Exam tip

Always read the question carefully. Check:
● Is it asking about the impact of legislation on service providers, practitioners or service users?
● Is the question asking about the impact of legislation generally or about the impact of a specific Act?

Revision activity

For each piece of legislation, write a list of impacts for service providers, care practitioners and service users. Use a sheet of A4 paper (landscape view) for each piece of legislation and add the information under three columns.

Common mistake

Writing about the impact of legislation generally, when the examination question requires the impact of a particular piece of legislation. Always read the question carefully before starting your answer!

Now test yourself

TESTED

1 Explain **one** impact of the Health and Safety at Work Act on practitioners and **one** impact on service users. [4]
2 State **two** key aspects of the Equality Act and explain how each aspect impacts on practitioners. [4]
3 Discuss the impact of legislation on service providers. [5]

Cambridge National Level 1/2 Health and Social Care 63

L04: Understand how personal hygiene, safety and security measures protect individuals

Personal hygiene measures

REVISED

There are many opportunities for bacteria to grow and infection to spread in health, social care and early years environments. A large number of individuals may use a care setting over the course of a day and many different activities take place, ranging from physical examinations at a GP surgery, treatments given at a hospital, to meals being prepared and served in a day centre or primary school. To prevent the spread of **infection** it is very important that everyone working in a care setting has a high standard of personal **hygiene**.

> **Infection**: when germs and bacteria invade the body and cause a disease or illness.
>
> **Hygiene**: practices that keep you and your surroundings clean in order to prevent illness and the spread of disease.

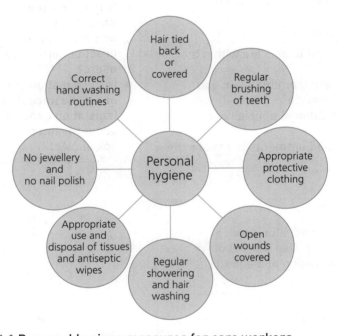

Figure 4.1 Personal hygiene measures for care workers

You can find further details of correct hand washing routines on pages 66 and 67. Information about the use of appropriate protective clothing in health, social care and early years settings is found on pages 68 and 69.

Personal hygiene rules when preparing and serving food
- Wash and dry hands thoroughly before and after touching food.
- Avoid coughing and sneezing near food; use a tissue if you need to cough or sneeze and dispose of it straightaway.
- Wash hands immediately after using a tissue and before touching any food or utensils.

> **Common mistake**
>
> **Mixing up personal hygiene with general cleanliness.** General cleanliness relates to the environment, whereas personal hygiene relates to the individual.

- Food should not be prepared by anyone who is unwell, for example, has diarrhoea or a cough or cold, as bacteria can easily spread to the food.
- Cuts and scratches should be covered with a coloured, waterproof plaster.
- Hair should be tied back or covered with a hairnet or food hygiene hat.
- A clean apron or overall should be worn to prevent bacteria from clothes coming into contact with food.

How good personal hygiene protects individuals

Good personal hygiene ensures a high level of individual cleanliness and helps stop the spread of infection between care workers and service users.

- Good personal hygiene prevents the transfer of **bacteria**.
- Thorough hand washing removes bacteria.
- Individuals who have regular showers (at least every other day) and clean their teeth regularly (every morning and evening) carry fewer bacteria, so reducing the risk of spreading infection.
- Barrier methods (protective clothing and covering wounds) help to reduce and prevent the transfer of bacteria (**cross-contamination**) and so the spread of infection.
- Jewellery can trap bacteria, so not wearing it removes the risk of bacteria being transferred from jewellery on the hands (for example, via rings and bracelets).
- Not wearing nail polish prevents **contamination**, as it could chip or flake off into food or into a patient's wound, for example.
- Tying hair back or covering it prevents it from dropping into food and contaminating it with any bacteria that are present.
- Using and disposing of tissues and antiseptic wipes appropriately prevents the spread of infection; this includes covering your mouth with a tissue when sneezing. Antiseptic wipes or hand gel can be a handy way of sterilising the skin to avoid the spread of infection. Special first aid antiseptic wipes are used for cleaning wounds such as minor cuts and scratches. All used wipes and tissues should be disposed of immediately after use into a covered bin.

> **Bacteria**: tiny, microscopic organisms. Some bacteria can cause infection and disease.
>
> **Cross-contamination**: when bacteria spreads onto food from another source, such as hands, work surfaces, kitchen equipment and utensils, or between cooked and raw food.
>
> **Contamination**: when something is tainted with other substances that may be unclean; for example, disease-causing bacteria.

Revision activity

Learn all of the examples of personal hygiene measures by making a copy of Figure 4.1. Then add to the diagram by writing a reason why each hygiene measure is important.

Now test yourself

TESTED ☐

1. Give the meaning of the term 'personal hygiene'. [1]
2. Explain why care workers should not wear jewellery or nail polish. [6]
3. Explain how good personal hygiene protects service users. [3]
4. Explain how good personal hygiene protects care workers. [3]
5. List **four** personal hygiene rules for someone working in a care setting. [4]

Hand washing routines

The most common way of spreading bacteria is by the hands. Germs accumulate on the hands as an individual touches surfaces, objects and people throughout the day. Frequent hand washing limits the transfer of bacteria and viruses and so reduces the chance of spreading infection. The correct technique to use for washing hands is shown in Figure 4.2.

Hand-washing technique with soap and water

Wet hands with water

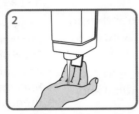

Apply enough soap to cover all hand surfaces

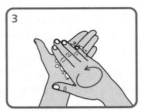

Rub hands palm to palm

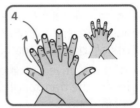

Rub back of each hand with palm of other hand with fingers interlaced

Rub palm to palm with fingers interlaced

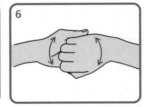

Rub with back of fingers to opposing palms with fingers interlocked

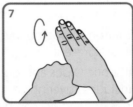

Rub each thumb clasped in opposite hand using a rotational movement

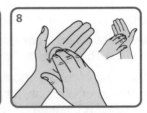

Rub tips of fingers in opposite palm in a circular motion

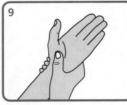

Rub each wrist with opposite hand

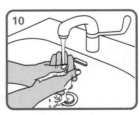

Rinse hands with water

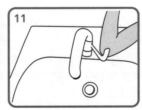

Use elbow to turn off tap

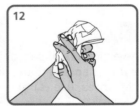

Dry thoroughly with a single-use towel

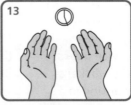

Hand washing should take 15–30 seconds

Figure 4.2 Hand washing procedure with soap and water

Note: Hands should always be dried thoroughly after washing.

Now test yourself answers at **www.hoddereducation.co.uk/myrevisionnotes**

When should care workers wash their hands?

- Before putting on and after removing disposable gloves.
- Before and after treating wounds or caring for a sick or injured person.
- Before and after providing personal care for an individual, such as feeding them or helping them get dressed.
- Before and after changing a nappy or incontinence pad.
- Before and after preparing or handling any food.
- After handling clinical waste.
- After clearing up rubbish and putting it in the bin.
- After clearing up toys or equipment.
- After using a tissue to blow your nose.
- After touching your face or hair.
- After using the toilet.

In an early years setting, staff set a good example for the children when they wash their hands regularly.

> **Revision activity**
>
> Create a flow chart showing the main stages for thorough hand washing.

> **Exam tip**
>
> Make sure that you know examples of when it is essential for care workers to wash their hands, as well as the reasons why it is necessary.

> **Common mistake**
>
> **Stating hands should be washed only 'after' a certain activity** when they need to be washed beforehand as well.

Now test yourself

TESTED ☐

1 Give **four** examples of occasions when care workers should wash their hands. [4]

2 Describe the correct routine for hand washing in a way that nursery age children can understand. [5]

3 Explain why thorough hand washing is very important in care settings. [6]

Protective clothing

Wearing protective clothing is a barrier method of preventing the spread of infection. The clothing can prevent the transfer of bacteria from a care worker to a service user and vice versa. (Protective clothing is sometimes referred to as PPE, which stands for 'personal protective equipment'.)

Appropriate protective clothing can include

- disposable aprons
- disposable gloves
- rubber gloves
- face masks
- hairnets or hygiene hats
- overalls
- overshoes
- surgical garments.

Figure 4.3 Examples of protective clothing used in a healthcare setting

Wearing disposable gloves

A fresh pair of disposable gloves should be used for each new task. Examples of when they should be worn are:

- changing nappies
- changing soiled bed linen
- dressing wounds
- clearing up spillages, such as vomit, blood
- food preparation and serving.

Wearing hairnets or hygiene hats (or tabards or overalls)

These are particularly important when preparing or serving food.

- If hair is not tied back or covered it is more likely to fall into food and staff are more likely to touch their hair. This can spread bacteria to food.
- Overalls or tabards provide a barrier covering the individual's clothes and so reduce the likelihood of transferring bacteria.

Now test yourself answers at **www.hoddereducation.co.uk/myrevisionnotes**

Wearing disposable aprons

A fresh apron should be used for each new task. Examples of when they should be worn are:

- bathing a service user
- changing soiled bed linen
- dressing wounds
- assisting someone with toileting
- putting on cream for someone who has an infectious skin condition
- dealing with incontinence pads.

Wearing face masks, surgical garments and overshoes

Face masks are effective barriers for droplets that can be released when talking, sneezing or coughing. Along with surgical garments and overshoes, they reduce the likelihood of contamination during procedures such as surgery or dental work.

Personal hygiene measures

Exam tip

Learn examples of protective clothing that could be used by care workers in different types of care settings. For each example, make sure you are able to give reasons for their use.

Common mistake

When identifying an example of protective clothing, do not just state 'gloves' or 'hat'. You need to be specific, for example 'a hygiene hat' or 'rubber gloves'.

Figure 4.4 Serving food in a primary school

Revision activity

Look carefully at Figure 4.3. Identify:
- each piece of protective clothing being used
- why it is being used
- how it protects the care worker sce users.

Now test yourself

TESTED

1. Identify **three** examples of protective clothing that could be worn by a care worker changing soiled bed sheets for a care home resident. [3]
2. Identify **three** tasks for which a care worker should wear disposable gloves. [3]
3. Give reasons why a hygiene hat would be worn. [2]
4. When and why would a face mask be worn? [2]
5. Look closely at Figure 4.4. Identify the protective clothing you can see and explain why it is good hygiene practice in a primary school. [6]

Safety procedures

A procedure is a process, not a specific action. It is a set of actions that are carried out in a particular order. A procedure informs care workers and service users about what they have to do and how it should be done to ensure everyone's safety; for example, how to arrange a safe school trip. Safety procedures are guidelines about how to deal with emergency situations such as fire.

Table 4.1 Safety procedures and how they protect individuals

Examples of safety procedures	How individuals are protected
• **Emergency evacuation procedure, practised with regular fire drills.** • **'Run, Hide, Tell' procedure for a terrorist attack.**	• ensures staff know their responsibilities in an emergency, enables them to take quick and efficient action • provides guidance for staff and service users to help keep them safe
• **DBS checks for all staff.** • **Safeguarding policy and procedures.**	• ensures checks are carried out so staff are safe to work with, for example, children and vulnerable adults, in care settings • staff are aware of safeguarding issues and what action to take
• **First aid policy and procedures.**	• appropriate treatment by trained staff
• **Food safety policy and procedures.**	• promotes good food hygiene practice • reduces the risk of food poisoning
• **Carrying out risk assessments for activities, outings and trips, equipment.**	• individuals are protected from avoidable injuries • equipment will be fit for purpose, no worn out or damaged equipment will be in use
• **Complying with the requirements of legislation – such as the Health and Safety at Work Act.**	• promotes good practice • ensures a safe environment for individuals in the care setting
• **Staff training – safeguarding, manual handling, first aid, etc.**	• alerts staff to potential dangers • enables staff to do their job safely • reduces risks and ensures a safer environment
• **Ensuring an appropriate staff to child ratio (or resident, patient etc.).**	• the level of supervision will be related to individual needs • improves the standard of care and safety levels

Safety measures

A safety measure is a specific action, such as:

● putting up a fire safety notice

● using a 'wet floor' sign after mopping the floor.

Figure 4.5 A wet floor sign is a safety measure

Table 4.2 Safety measures and how they protect individuals

Examples of safety measures	How individuals are protected
• Fire safety notices in every room in the care setting. • Signs indicating fire exits and assembly points. • Fire doors kept clear. • A fire extinguisher available by each external exit. • A fire blanket available in kitchen areas. • Fire alarms throughout the building.	• Promotes awareness of safety procedures. • Informs care workers and service users where to go and what to do in an emergency. • Helps to keep staff and service users safe.
Safety warning signs such as: • careful – wet floor • no smoking • danger: corrosive • no entry.	• Raises awareness of possible hazards. • Helps prevent accidents.
Wearing protective clothing.	• Wearing items such as goggles prevents injury. • Aprons, disposable gloves and so on, help prevent the spread of infection.

Revision activity

Produce two concept maps: one for safety measures, the other for safety procedures. Include examples of how they protect individuals.

Exam tip

Make sure that you know examples of safety 'measures' and safety 'procedures' and can explain how they protect care workers and service users.

Common mistake

Mixing up 'security measures' with 'safety measures'. Remember that a procedure is a process that is followed such as a fire drill, whereas a measure is a particular action such as putting up a wet floor sign.

Now test yourself

TESTED ☐

1 Explain the difference between a safety 'measure' and a safety 'procedure'. [2]
2 Describe **four** ways nursery staff could ensure a safe environment for the children. [8]
3 What are 'DBS checks'? [3]
4 Give **three** benefits of having regular fire drills in a care setting. [3]
5 State **two** benefits of providing staff with training in safety procedures. [2]

Emergency procedures

Fire procedures

Every care setting is required to have a fire emergency evacuation plan that includes the action to be taken by all staff in the event of a fire. An example evacuation procedure for a nursing home is shown in Figure 4.6.

Fire safety measures include:

- fire safety notices throughout the care setting
- signs indicating fire exits and assembly points
- a fire extinguisher by each exit
- a fire blanket in kitchen areas.

Fire drills should be practised regularly – at least once a year – so that staff and service users are fully aware of the procedures to follow. New staff should be trained when they start work.

Checkleigh Nursing Home

Fire evacuation procedure

- If you discover a fire, raise the alarm – alert people in the immediate area, activate alarm system, call 999.
- All staff to remove people from their immediate area – direct them to the fire assembly point, use designated fire exits, never use lifts.
- Designated staff assist residents with:
  - mobility difficulties (use of evac chairs/wheelchairs)
  - hearing difficulties (may not hear alarm)
  - dementia patients (may be confused/unaware of what is happening).
- Staff to close doors and windows, switch off lights as they leave.
- Staff evacuating the building must check their locality is clear.
- Everyone to assemble at designated external assembly point to await further instructions.
- Do not re-enter the building until told it is safe to do so.
- Carry out head count to ensure everyone is accounted for.
- Senior staff to inform fire brigade if anyone is left in the building

---

Figure 4.6 Example of a nursing home fire evacuation procedure

Evacuation procedures

Emergency events – such as a gas leak, flood or bomb threat – require a setting to be evacuated quickly and efficiently to keep people safe.

In the very rare event of a firearms or weapons attack, the government has provided advice on how individuals can keep themselves safe. Leaflets, posters and films are available.

Care settings are encouraged to ensure they raise awareness of this advice sensitively, particularly with children.

- **Run** – if you can
- **Hide** – if you can't run away, and
- **Tell** – the police, when it is safe to do so.

First aid

In case of health emergencies, care settings must have enough trained first aiders available for the number of staff and service users. The health needs of the service users would also be taken into account.

Figure 4.7 Stay safe advice

Now test yourself answers at www.hoddereducation.co.uk/myrevisionnotes

First aiders must:

- be trained
- have up-to-date knowledge.

Some staff should be trained in how to use an **Epipen**, based on an assessment of the number of individuals in a care setting who are at risk of **anaphylactic shock**.

How emergency procedures protect individuals

- Ensure that everyone is kept as safe as possible and away from danger.
- Ensure the care setting complies with health and safety legislation.
- Provide guidance for staff so they know exactly what to do in an emergency.
- Enable staff to take quick and efficient action to remove service users and themselves from danger.
- Provide guidance for service users so they know what to do in an emergency.
- Individuals using services will be reassured by knowing these procedures exist to help them in an emergency.
- Awareness that staff are trained to deal with emergency situations reduces anxiety for service users and instils trust.

> **Epipen**: an emergency treatment for someone with a severe anaphylactic reaction. It is an automatic injector device that contains a dose of the hormone adrenaline, which is injected into the thigh.
>
> **Anaphylactic shock**: an extreme allergic reaction. Common causes can be nuts, celery, seafood, and wasp or bee stings.

> **Revision activity**
>
> Read the nursing home fire evacuation procedure, shown in Figure 4.6. For each of the bullet points, explain how the action described protects individuals.

> **Exam tip**
>
> Make sure you can give specific examples of emergency procedures and reasons why they protect care workers and service users.

> **Common mistake**
>
> **Mixing up 'fire procedures' and 'fire safety measures'.** Make sure that you know the difference: having a fire evacuation plan in place is a procedure; putting a fire extinguisher by a doorway is a fire safety measure.

Now test yourself

TESTED ☐

1. List **four** points that should be included in a care setting fire evacuation procedure. [4]
2. Discuss how the fire evacuation procedure shown in Figure 4.6 benefits both service users and service providers. [8]
3. State **four** safety measures that a Day Centre should have in place to protect individuals using the care setting. [4]
4. How would a care setting work out the number of trained first aiders they need? [2]

Equipment considerations

Care workers in health, social care and early years settings will use a range of equipment with service users, ranging from mobility aids and manual handling equipment to toys and household appliances.

Staff training

Staff should be appropriately trained to use specialist equipment such as:

- hoists
- transfer boards
- slings
- slide sheets
- leg-lifters
- fire evacuation chairs.

Equipment safety

- Nursery toys should be checked for small or loose components that could be choking hazards.
- Nursery toys should be age appropriate.
- All equipment and toys in care settings should have appropriate safety labels. Examples of safety labels are shown in Figure 4.8.

Figure 4.8 The BSI, Lion Mark and age advice safety symbols

Equipment should be fit for purpose

- Equipment should be appropriate for the task being carried out and in good condition.
- Specialist equipment should be available if needed; for example, to assist individuals to move from a wheelchair into a bath.
- Equipment should be maintained in good working order; for example, hoists serviced regularly.

Regular maintenance checks

Regular maintenance checks should be carried out to ensure:

- faults are spotted early
- repairs are carried out as soon as they are needed
- any damaged items, such as toys, wheelchairs, safety gates and so on, are disposed of or repaired, as appropriate
- electrical equipment is PAT tested annually and taken out of use if not safe.

Care settings should also have:

- a reporting system for damaged or faulty equipment
- a replacement programme for older or worn-out equipment.

How equipment considerations improve safety

- Damage is spotted early before anyone is injured.
- Correct equipment is provided for the task.
- Staff are trained and know how to use the equipment correctly, so preventing injuries to themselves or service users.
- Specialist equipment is available when needed – for example, hoists, fire evacuation chairs and so on – so that service users are moved safely.
- Electrical equipment is safe so the risk of injury is reduced.
- Ensures the care setting is complying with health and safety legislation.

> **Exam tip**
>
> Make sure that you can explain how equipment considerations improve safety in care settings. Be able to give examples to develop your explanation.

> **Revision activity**
>
> Make a list of equipment used in a children's nursery. Write an explanation of the equipment considerations that should be in place so that a safe standard of care is provided.
> Then repeat this task for:
> - a hospital
> - a nursing home.

> **Common mistake**
>
> **Giving answers relating only to specialist equipment in care settings, such as hoists.** Don't forget to include everyday items such as televisions, toasters and hairdryers in a residential care home – or scissors and toys in a nursery, for example.

Now test yourself

TESTED ☐

1 How could a nursery manager ensure that toys purchased for use in the nursery are safe? [2]
2 Explain how having a reporting system for damaged or faulty equipment could help protect care workers and service users. [6]
3 What is PAT testing? [2]
4 Outline how equipment considerations improve safety in care settings. [4]

Moving and handling techniques

Care workers often have to move items of equipment, trolleys, boxes of toys, tables and chairs, and sometimes have to physically assist individuals to move. It is essential that anyone who has to move or handle as part of their job role is trained to do so properly. Individuals receiving care or the care worker may be injured if the care worker attempts manual handling incorrectly.

The Manual Handling Operations Regulations (1992) define manual handling as 'any transporting of a load including lifting, putting down, pushing, pulling, carrying or moving' of the load. A load can be a person or an object.

Situations when moving and handling might be necessary

- Transferring a patient from a hospital bed to a chair.
- Assisting an elderly person with their mobility; for example, helping them to get out of a chair or into a bath or shower.
- Arranging tables and chairs in a nursery.
- Carrying boxes of toys.
- Pushing trolleys, drip stands, wheelchairs and so on.
- Moving a commode into an elderly person's bedroom.
- A home care assistant carrying shopping bags.

Figure 4.9 A nurse using a hoist to move a patient

Moving people

It is important to use effective communication skills to tell the person what you are going to do in a way that they will understand. Always ask the person for their permission to carry out the move.

When moving people:

- bend your knees not your back
- avoid twisting the back, as this can cause damage to the spine
- use the specialist equipment provided.

Moving objects

- Only move objects if really necessary.
- Only lift as much as can be easily carried – do not lift as much as you can, as this can cause injury much more easily.
- Check that there are no dangers in the environment, such as an uneven or slippery floor, and that there is enough space to carry out the move.
- Bend the knees and avoid twisting the back or moving sideways.
- Keep feet wide apart for stability.
- Hold the item being lifted close to the body.
- Move smoothly not jerkily; this reduces the risk of injury.
- Use appropriate equipment, such as a trolley or a box on wheels.
- Shopping should be split between two bags and carried one in each hand to spread the load.

Safe manual handling

- Always check whether the move or lift is really necessary. Do not carry out a move unless it is unavoidable.
- Identify any risks involved in carrying out the move and take steps to avoid or minimise the risks identified.

- Use a lifting aid if appropriate, rather than carrying out the lift yourself.
- If the move has been assessed to require two people, do not attempt the move on your own.
- Only carry out manual handing if you have been trained to do so.

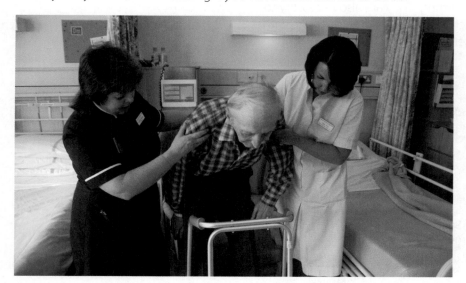

Figure 4.10 Moving and handling individuals often requires two people

How correct moving and handling techniques protect individuals

- Manual handling training provides staff with guidance on good practice so they know how to lift and move individuals safely and with confidence.
- Risks to service users and staff will be assessed and minimised.
- Staff will know if a second person is needed for the manual handling task.
- Staff will do their job correctly, so ensuring a safer working environment.
- Service users will have more confidence in staff who have been trained in manual handling, which will help them relax when being moved because they trust the staff to do their job well.
- It prevents injuries to both service users and care workers.
- Being trained protects staff from accusations of abuse, as when correct techniques are used, service users will feel comfortable and that they are being treated with dignity and respect.

Exam tip

You need to be able to give examples of correct moving and handling techniques and how these protect care workers and service users.

Common mistake

Not mentioning that moving and handling has to be risk assessed and that two people who are both trained are often needed to carry out the move.

Revision activity

Produce an information sheet for a care assistant in a residential care home, with key instructions about moving people safely.

Now test yourself   TESTED ☐

1 Identify **four** situations when moving and handling might be necessary. [4]
2 Why is it important to use effective communication skills to explain to an individual that they are going to be moved in a hoist like the one in Figure 4.9? [5]
3 Give the correct procedure for safely moving a box of toys. [6]
4 State **three** ways of ensuring safe manual handling. [3]
5 State **three** ways care workers are protected by using correct manual handling techniques. [3]

Security measures

Security measures in heath, social care and early years settings are necessary to keep staff and service users safe; for example, by stopping unauthorised individuals from entering the care setting. They are also necessary to prevent vulnerable individuals, such as young children or adults with dementia, from leaving the care setting unsupervised.

Figure 4.11 Examples of security measures in care settings

How security measures protect individuals

Table 4.3 Security of people

Examples of security measures	How individuals are protected
• Staff on duty at the reception desk. • Signing in and out book for visitors. • Escorting visitors into and off the premises.	• Individuals must register before being allowed into the setting; this identifies who they are. • Controls access to the setting – only authorised people allowed in. • Staff know who is in the care setting and why they are there and where they are at all times. • In a nursery, children will only be released to authorised people, for example, those with a password.
• Issuing visitor badges. • Staff wearing ID lanyards. • Staff uniform.	• Easy to spot unauthorised people as lanyards and/or uniforms quickly identify staff. • Easy to identify visitors.
• Reporting of concerns to managers.	• Raises management awareness of security breaches. • Appropriate action can be initiated by senior staff to address security issues.

Table 4.4 Security of the building

Examples of security measures	How individuals are protected
• Having a staff member with responsibility for monitoring and checking external entrances. • Having a member of staff on duty at the reception desk.	• Controls access to the building. • Only allows authorised individuals to enter the care setting. • Prevents residents, patients, toddlers or children wandering out of the care setting.
• Locks on external doors. • Monitoring of keys.	• A limited number of people will have keys so access is controlled. • Having a list of key holders means the whereabouts of all sets of keys is known at all times. • Prevents intruders from entering the building.
• Security pads with pin codes. • Electronic swipe card entry system. • Buzzer entry system.	• Restricts access to authorised people. • Prevents vulnerable service users wandering out of the care setting. • Prevents strangers and intruders from gaining access to the setting.
• CCTV monitoring exits and entrances. • Alarms on external doors that are not in regular use.	• Monitors staff and visitors accessing the building. • Alarms identify if anyone is going in or out unannounced.
• Window locks and window restraints.	• Prevents unwanted visitors getting into the setting. • Keeps vulnerable individuals safe by preventing them from, for example, falling through an open window or leaving the care setting unattended.

Security measures (side tab)

Exam tip

Give precise examples of security measures to achieve more marks; for example, you could suggest 'have a manned reception desk' rather than 'have a reception desk'; 'have a signing in and out book for visitors' not 'have a logbook'; 'have CCTV cameras to monitor the main external doors', not 'have cameras in all the rooms'.

Revision activity

Learn all of the examples of security measures by making a copy of Figure 4.11. Then extend the diagram by writing an explanation of how each measure protects individuals in care settings.

Common mistake

Giving vague explanations of security measures; for example, that all doors should be locked in a care setting to keep people safe. This would not be appropriate as it is not acceptable to lock individuals into rooms in a care setting. To prevent unauthorised access you could state that all external doors should be locked and have a buzzer so that only the receptionist can allow visitors to enter; alternatively you could suggest that the main entrance is accessed via an electronic key pad only.

Now test yourself

TESTED ☐

1 Explain the benefits of wearing staff lanyards and visitor badges in a care setting. [6]

2 State **four** ways staff at a nursing home could ensure that the building is secure. [4]

3 Describe **four** ways nursery staff could ensure security for the children. [4]

4 How does monitoring keys help to provide security in a care setting? [3]

Methods for reducing spread of infection: General cleanliness

Different care settings will have different types of furniture and equipment, and the methods of maintaining general cleanliness will vary, depending on the setting and the type of care services provided. Some examples of how to maintain a high standard of general cleanliness are listed below.

General cleanliness in healthcare settings

- Clear spillages, for example, vomit, urine, blood, straightaway then clean and disinfect the area.
- Sterilise surgical equipment after use.
- Dispose of hazardous waste following correct procedures; for example, dispose of hospital **sharps** (needles, **cannulas**) in a hard yellow sharps box.
- Provide specialist disposal methods, such as red laundry bags for soiled bed linen and yellow bags for used dressings, disposable gloves and other clinical waste.
- Clean and disinfect bathrooms and toilets frequently (at least once daily).
- All used antiseptic wipes and tissues should be disposed of immediately after use into a covered bin.

> **Sharps**: items of equipment with sharp points that can puncture or cut the skin; examples include needles and cannulas.
>
> **Cannulas**: thin tubes that surround a flexible needle that is inserted into a vein to administer medication from a drip.

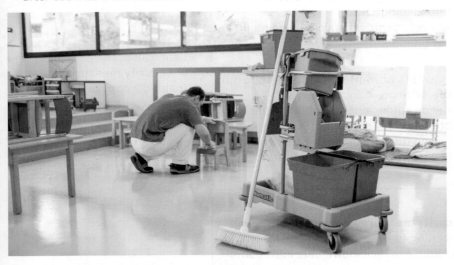

Figure 4.12 Thorough cleaning is a high priority in care settings to help prevent the spread of infection

General cleanliness in early years settings

- Use anti-bacterial sprays or wipes on work surfaces, door handles and computer keyboards.
- Clean toys and play equipment regularly.
- Clean and disinfect toilets frequently, at least daily.
- Mop floors and vacuum carpets every day.
- Empty and clean bins frequently.

General cleanliness in social care settings

- Mop floors and vacuum carpets every day.
- Wash work surfaces with hot soapy water.
- Use bins with lids; bins should be emptied and cleaned frequently.

- Clean and disinfect bathrooms and toilets frequently, at least daily.
- Wash bedding and towels regularly. Put soiled bedding into special red laundry bags.
- Wash curtains, blinds and soft furnishings (such as cushion covers) regularly.
- Dust coffee tables, dining tables and chairs regularly.
- TV remote controls and computer keyboards should be cleaned and anti-bacterial spray used.

How general cleanliness helps to prevent the spread of infection

- Prevents transfer of bacteria from surfaces or between care workers, service users, visitors and families.
- Destroys bacteria.
- Barrier methods reduce or prevent the likely transfer of bacteria.
- Reduces places where bacteria can be trapped.
- Ensures a high standard of hygiene.
- Reduces the opportunities for spreading bacteria.
- Stops others from coming into contact with bacteria, so reducing cross-infection.

Figure 4.13 All surfaces and equipment need to be cleaned regularly

Exam tip

Always read the question carefully. Often, exam questions will be set in the context of a specific care setting. Check: is the question asking about hygiene in a health, social care or early years setting? Make sure your answer relates to the correct type of setting.

Revision activity

Produce a spider diagram for each type of care setting (health, social care, early years). Include as many ways as you can of maintaining good standards of hygiene and cleanliness in each type of setting.

Common mistake

Giving vague answers. For example, if you are asked how a care worker can maintain high standards of cleanliness in a care setting, stating 'keep everything clean'. This would not gain marks and it lacks detail. To gain higher marks your answer should include some specific ways of keeping the environment clean, such as vacuuming carpets every day or washing down work surfaces with hot soapy water.

Now test yourself
TESTED

1 Identify **three** ways a GP surgery could ensure high standards of general cleanliness. [3]
2 Look closely at Figure 4.12. Identify and explain the good hygiene practices you can see. [4]
3 Describe how a high standard of general cleanliness could be maintained in a nursery. [6]
4 Figure 4.13 shows a desk and computer being cleaned. Give reasons why this is important in the following care settings: on a hospital ward and in the residents' lounge at a retirement home. [4]

Methods for reducing spread of infection: Food hygiene in care settings

Many care settings such as hospitals, nursing and retirement homes, day centres and nurseries, prepare and provide meals for their service users.

Following correct food hygiene procedures can help to prevent cross-contamination and outbreaks of food poisoning. For some groups of individuals who use care services, food poisoning can be very serious. These 'at risk' groups are:

● babies and young children
● pregnant women
● elderly people
● people with reduced immunity.

There are many ways food can become contaminated. Bacteria can enter food during:

● storage
● preparation
● cooking
● serving.

Figure 4.14 shows some of the main causes of food contamination.

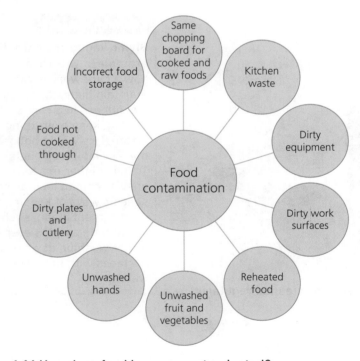

Figure 4.14 How does food become contaminated?

Food hygiene measures
● Wash your hands thoroughly before any food preparation.
● Ensure all work surfaces and equipment are clean before preparing food.
● Wipe clean surfaces with a clean cloth soaked in hot water and **anti-bacterial** washing-up liquid.
● After wiping down surfaces, use an anti-bacterial spray – these do not remove grease and dirt, so should be used after cleaning.
● Wash fruit and vegetables before use.

Anti-bacterial: something that destroys bacteria or prevents their growth.

- Use different coloured chopping boards when preparing meals to keep raw and cooked food separate and avoid cross-contamination, which could lead to food poisoning.

The different coloured boards to use are:
- white – bread and dairy
- red – raw meat and poultry
- yellow – cooked meat
- brown – vegetables
- blue – fish
- green – salad and fruit
- Clear away used equipment and spilt food as you work.
- Use correct food storage methods; for example, put fresh meat and fish on the bottom shelf in the fridge; ensure cooked food is cool before freezing.
- Check and follow 'use by' and 'eat by' dates.
- Cook food thoroughly to kill bacteria – a food temperature probe or meat thermometer should be used to check that food has reached 75°C or above.
- Keep food covered; for example, with cling film, foil or in a lidded container, to prevent contamination.
- Serve food as soon as it is cooked, so that bacteria do not have time to multiply.

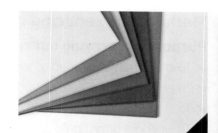

Figure 4.15 Colour-coded chopping boards can help to prevent cross-contamination

Exam tip

You need to learn the procedures for food hygiene and be able to give reasons for them.

Common mistake

Making vague statements instead of giving specific food hygiene procedures; for example, stating 'keep everything clean' without saying how to do this and why.

Revision activity

Make a copy of Figure 4.14 then extend it by writing a way of avoiding each of the causes of food contamination shown.

Now test yourself
TESTED ☐

1 List **four** kitchen hygiene rules for preparing food in a care setting. [4]
2 State **four** personal hygiene rules for someone involved in preparing and serving food in a care setting. [4]
3 Which groups of people are most at risk of serious illness as a result of food poisoning? [4]
4 How do colour-coded chopping boards help prevent cross-contamination? [3]
5 At what temperature is food thoroughly cooked? [1]

Methods for reducing risk/danger: Risk assessment

Purpose of carrying out risk assessments

✔ To check that equipment is safe and fit for purpose.

✔ To ensure that the care setting building is safe.

✔ To identify potential dangers, such as trip hazards, risky activities.

✔ To work out what could go wrong with an activity.

✔ To assess how much supervision is needed.

✔ To identify ways of controlling and minimising **risks**.

✔ To ensure any planned trips or visits are safe to proceed.

Reasons for carrying out risk assessments

- It is a legal requirement under the Health and Safety at Work Act. The written record provides evidence that the **risk assessments** have been carried out.

- Staff, service users and visitors have a right to be protected and kept safe from harm.

- To identify any **hazards** that could cause harm to people using the care setting.

- To prevent accidents, illness and danger.

- Staff, service users and visitors will feel confident using the service knowing that risk assessments are carried out.

Types of hazards in care settings

- Trip hazards such as rugs, trailing cables, toys on the floor, wet floors.

- Blocked fire exits.

- Lack of security.

- Unsafe storage of hazardous substances, for example, cleaning materials, chemicals and medication should all be kept locked away.

- Inadequate supervision.

- Unsafe, faulty or worn out equipment, such as a hoist that has not been serviced or maintained for a couple of years, or toys that have small, loose parts.

- Unsafe soft furnishings or furniture, such as a frayed rug or wobbly table.

> **Risk**: the likelihood that someone or something could be harmed.
>
> **Risk assessment**: the process of evaluating the likelihood of a hazard actually causing harm.
>
> **Hazard**: anything that could cause harm.
>
> **Control measures**: actions that can be taken to reduce the risks posed by hazards or to remove hazards altogether.

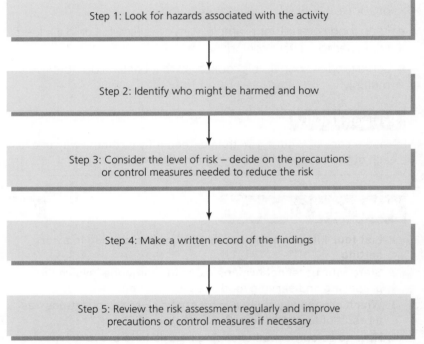

Step 1: Look for hazards associated with the activity

Step 2: Identify who might be harmed and how

Step 3: Consider the level of risk – decide on the precautions or control measures needed to reduce the risk

Step 4: Make a written record of the findings

Step 5: Review the risk assessment regularly and improve precautions or control measures if necessary

Figure 4.16 Carrying out a risk assessment involves the five steps shown

The importance of risk assessments

- Risk assessment is a legal requirement. In settings with more than five employees, all risk assessments must be recorded.

- Their purpose is to reduce the risk of harm to service users, visitors and staff.

- Staff must identify potential hazards; for example, by taking a walk around the setting looking for things that may cause harm to patients, small children or staff, such as faulty electrical equipment.

Now test yourself answers at **www.hoddereducation.co.uk/myrevisionnotes**

- Staff must identify potential hazards that may occur during planned activities or outings with adults and children; for example, using scissors for cutting out with inadequate staff supervision, lack of wheelchair access, trip hazards and so on.
- When potential hazards in the setting are identified, action must be taken so that accidents and harm are avoided.

Table 4.5 Example risk assessment for Willowfield Residential Home

Activity	Hazards identified	Control measures required	Level of risk	Date for review
Transferring Mrs Smith from her wheelchair into the bath	• Broken hoist. • Possible lifting injuries – bruising, muscle strain or worse.	• Equipment log book, to record any damage to equipment – to be checked daily. • Maintenance book, to ensure that equipment is regularly checked.	High	Weekly
Fire drill	• Wheelchairs stored in front of fire doors – delaying access to fire door.	• Arrange for wheelchair storage away from the fire exit. • Use of folding wheelchairs for safer storage.	High	Weekly
Residents' art class	• Spillages – water and paint on the floor. • Trip hazard – risk of falls causing sprains, bruising, broken limbs.	• Supervision – one additional member of staff to assist residents. • Cleaner available during the class to mop up spills straightaway.	Medium	At each class

Exam tip

You need to be able to describe the purpose of carrying out risk assessments and how to identify hazards in care settings, and explain ways of reducing the risks (control measures).

Common mistake

Mixing up 'risk' and 'hazard'. Be clear about the difference: a hazard is something that could cause harm; a risk is the likelihood of harm occurring, so a hazard can be low, medium or high risk.

Revision activity

Copy out and add to Table 4.5 by carrying out a risk assessment for each of the following:
- cutting and sticking activity in a primary classroom
- vacuuming the residents' lounge in a retirement home
- giving medication to a hospital patient.

Now test yourself

TESTED ☐

1 What is the difference between a hazard and a risk? [2]
2 What is a 'control measure'? [1]
3 Explain the five stages of a risk assessment. [8]
4 Identify **three** possible hazards in a nursery. [3]

Procedures to prevent accidents and promote good practice

Accident prevention

The most common types of accidents in any workplace are slips, trips and falls. Figure 4.17 shows some ways to avoid this type of accident.

The second most common type of accident is muscle strains from manual handling. This type of injury can be avoided if staff are trained to carry out manual handling correctly. Different types of care setting have potentially different types of accidents; for example, the likelihood of a **sharps injury** is higher in a hospital than in a nursery.

> **Sharps injury**: when the skin is punctured by a needle or blade, such as a scalpel or other medical instrument.

Figure 4.17 Ways of preventing slips, trips and falls in care settings

Staff training

One of the best ways to minimise the risk of accidents and to promote good practice is to train staff. Staff training raises awareness and develops knowledge and skills. It means staff then know which policies and procedures to follow to prevent accidents in the care setting, and will be aware of their specific roles and responsibilities.

Training enables staff to:

- develop the skills and knowledge to avoid injuries to themselves and service users
- gain awareness of security measures used to keep individuals safe
- understand how to apply the values of care
- develop knowledge of effective communication
- carry out first aid
- understand safeguarding procedures
- have knowledge of health and safety policies and procedures
- carry out risk assessments
- carry out moving and handling techniques safely.

Policies

All health, social care and early years settings have policies in place. A policy is a plan that outlines the policy purpose and the instructions for carrying out the necessary actions to achieve its aim of keeping service users safe and promoting their rights. Policies also ensure that the care setting is complying with the requirements of legislation.

Example policies found in care settings include:

- accident reporting
- bullying
- confidentiality
- equal opportunities
- fire evacuation
- health and safety
- manual handling
- risk assessment
- safeguarding.

Risk assessment

The aim of carrying out risk assessments is to identify potential risks to the health, safety and security of care workers, service users and visitors to a care setting. Some activities, equipment and care provided in care settings can be hazardous, but the aim of a risk assessment is to identify ways that the risks can be minimised or removed completely.

> **Exam tip**
>
> Make sure you know examples of procedures, information and guidelines that help prevent accidents and promote good practice.

Figure 4.18 Use the acronym 'PIG' to help you remember ways to prevent accidents and promote good practice

> **Revision activity**
>
> To help you remember ways to prevent accidents and promote good practice, use the acronym **PIG**:
> - **P**rocedures
> - **I**nformation
> - **G**uidelines.
>
> For example:
> - **Procedures:** fire drill, evacuation plan, risk assessment, accident procedure.
> - **Information:** escape route map in case of fire, wet floor sign, fire exit sign, staff training.
> - **Guidelines:** manual handling policy, health and safety policy, food hygiene measures.

Now test yourself

TESTED ☐

1 Name **two** procedures that should be followed in a care setting. [2]
2 State the benefits for care workers of following the two procedures you named in Question 1. [2]
3 Describe **three** benefits of providing staff with training. [6]
4 Identify **three** policies that should be in place in a care setting. [3]

Success in the examination

The written exam

Unit R021 is an examined unit where you will sit an examination paper that is set and marked by the OCR examinations board.

In the examination you will be tested on four Learning Objectives (LOs):

- L01 – Understand how to support individuals to maintain their rights.
- L02 – Understand the importance of the values of care and how they are applied.
- L03 – Understand how legislation impacts on care settings.
- L04 – Understand how personal hygiene, safety and security measures protect individuals.

Questions might be about a particular LO topic or might require answers that combine information from two or more different LOs.

When can the examination be taken?

The R021 examination is available in both the January and June sessions. You can sit the examination in Year 10 or Year 11. Most students will sit the examination in Year 11.

How long will I have to complete the exam?

The examination length is one hour.

What type of questions will appear in the exam paper?

You can expect to find a wide range of different types of questions on the paper, for example:

- some 1-mark questions requiring a one-word answer
- multiple choice questions
- short answer questions worth 2 to 4 marks
- longer extended response questions worth 5 to 8 marks.

None of the individual parts of a question will be worth more than 8 marks.

You have to answer all of the questions.

Structure of the question paper

The examination paper is worth 60 marks.

- **Section A** = 34 marks.
- **Section B** = 26 marks.

Now test yourself answers at www.hoddereducation.co.uk/myrevisionnotes

What is the difference between Section A and Section B?

Section A	Section B
• There are three questions in Section A. • Each question is context based. This means it will be about a scenario in a specific health, social care or early years setting. The scenarios will be different every exam session. • Example settings could include: a GP surgery, a nursing home, a day centre, a hospital, a shelter for the homeless, a retirement home, a nursery, a playgroup or a primary school. • You will need to apply your knowledge of the RO21 topics to produce an answer that is relevant to the scenario you are given.	• There are two questions in Section B. • The questions in Section B are fact and knowledge based. You will not have to give answers based on any particular care setting.

Command verbs

REVISED

All of the questions will have a 'command verb'. This will tell you what you have to do to answer the question. Examples of command verbs, starting with the easiest to the more demanding, are shown in the table.

Command verbs	Meaning
Identify	Give brief information or facts such as naming, stating or listing who or what something is. Often one-word answers.
Outline	Give the main, key aspects or facts about something.
Describe	Give an account that includes all of the relevant facts, features, qualities or aspects of something.
Explain	Provide more depth and detail than a description. You will include relevant reasons for, purposes of, or effects of something.
Analyse	Separate information into components and examine it methodically and in detail, in order to explain and interpret it.
Discuss	Give an account that considers a range of ideas and viewpoints.
Assess	Give a reasoned judgement or opinion of the quality, standard or effectiveness of something, informed by relevant facts.
Evaluate	Make a judgement about something by taking into account different factors and including strengths and weaknesses/positives and negatives.

Always check the command verb carefully before answering a question. If you describe something when an explanation is required, you will not be able to gain full marks. This is because an explanation requires more detail than a description.

Exam technique – top tips!

There is more to producing a good answer to an exam question than simply knowing the facts. The quality of your response, such as how you organise your answer and whether it is fully relevant to the question, all help you gain extra marks.

- Read each question through carefully at least twice before you start your answer.
- Underline or highlight the command verb, so that you are clear about what you have to do.
- If a question asks for 'ways', without saying how many ways, you must give a minimum of two as 'ways' is plural. The same rule applies to 'methods', 'reasons' and so on.
- For higher mark questions (worth 5–8 marks) write your answer in paragraphs. Each paragraph should focus on a specific aspect of the answer. This ensures your answer is organised and logical.
- Make sure the information in your answer is accurate and relevant to the question – don't just write everything you know about a topic – stay focused and answer the question!
- Be guided by the number of marks and space provided for the length of your answer. The more marks, the more space will be provided. Unless you have very large handwriting, you should not need to continue your answer onto the extra pages at the end of the examination paper.
- If you do continue your answers on the extra pages, make sure you state the question number and the part of the question, such as 3(b) or 6(a), so that the examiner marking your paper knows exactly which question you are answering.
- Do not leave any questions unanswered. Even if you feel you don't know the answer, have go – you probably know more than you think you do!

Preparing for the exam

- Find the past papers and mark schemes on the OCR website. Have a go at a paper then mark it yourself using the mark scheme.
- Always ask your teacher if you don't understand something or are not sure – your teacher is there to help you.
- It is never too early to start revising: begin your revision by going through your handouts and notes after each lesson – don't just file them away!
- Remember: the more times you go through a topic, the more you will remember it.
- Make a revision plan that includes a timetable with dates. You can use the revision planner at the front of this book and tick off each topic after you have revised it.
- Use the revision activities suggested in this book, so that you don't get bored just reading through notes all the time.
- Learn the key terms for each topic, so that you are able to correctly use specialist terminology in your answers.

Sample practice questions and commentary

Section A: Context-based questions

Section A: Sample question 1

Mrs Smith is in hospital. She will be having treatment for her stomach problems. Consultation is one of the rights Mrs Smith is entitled to.

Explain **two** ways that the doctor looking after Mrs Smith could support her right to consultation. [4 marks]

Response 1: High level response – total 4/4 marks

> 1 The doctor could tell Mrs Smith all the details of the different possible treatment options available for her condition. This information would enable her to choose which treatment she wished to receive, rather than just being told how she is going to be treated.
>
> 2 The doctor could listen to Mrs Smith's views, answer her questions and discuss with her the best type of treatment. This supports her right to consultation because she will feel her opinions are valued and that she is more in control of what is happening.

Response 2: Mid level response – total 2/4 marks

> 1 The doctor could tell Mrs Smith about the best treatment for her illness and answer questions she might have.
>
> 2 The doctor could allow her to discuss her treatment.

Commentary

Question context and requirements:

- The scenario context is based on a hospital patient.
- Two 'ways' are required.
- An 'explanation' includes relevant reasons for and purposes of the ways that support the right to consultation.
- Two marks for each 'way' explained.
- This question is assessed against LO1: Understand how to support individuals to maintain their rights.

Response 1: 4/4 marks

- Two ways are given, both are appropriate and in the hospital context.
- There is good use of appropriate terminology throughout, such as 'options', 'opinions', 'discuss' and 'valued'.
- Each answer provides a 'way' which is followed by 'explanation' of how it supports consultation.
- Both answers show clear knowledge and understanding of what consultation involves.

Response 2: 2/4 marks

- Two ways are given: providing information about the best treatment and discussing the treatment. These are both correct and gained one mark each.

- Links to supporting consultation have not been made, as the response does not, for example, provide an explanation about how the ways given empower Mrs Smith or make her feel valued.

Mark scheme

Ways the doctor could support the right to consultation:	Explanation of how the ways support Mrs Smith's right to consultation:
• telling Mrs Smith about the range of treatments available for her condition • asking Mrs Smith for her opinion about different treatments • explaining what each type of treatment will involve • explaining the advantages and disadvantages of the different treatments.	• she will feel valued • she will feel listened to • she will feel empowered and in control of what is happening to her • she will be able to make an informed choice • her views and opinions will be taken in account by the doctor.

[4 marks]

Section A: Sample question 2

Samira is the headteacher of a primary school. She wants her school to provide every child with the best opportunities to achieve their full potential.

Describe how Samira could apply the early years value of care '**ensuring equality of opportunity**' in her day-to-day work with the children.

[8 marks]

Response 1: High level response – total 8/8 marks

Samira could ensure that her school provides access to all areas and activities for all of the children. This would include providing ramps for children who use a wheelchair so that they can access the whole building and all the play areas. It could also include providing worksheets in large print for those with visual impairments, having a member of staff who can do British Sign Language, or providing a hearing loop system for those with hearing impairments. The school could provide teaching assistants to support children who have physical or learning disabilities. One-to-one support would enable them to make progress and would meet their individual needs so that they are not disadvantaged.

As headteacher, Samira should ensure that the school has policies in place, such as 'Equal Opportunities', 'Bullying' and 'Safeguarding'. If all the staff are trained about the policies they will be aware of how to promote equal opportunities in their work and how to challenge discriminatory behaviour. They will ensure the children know about the policies too. This means that any child who is not being treated fairly, or is being bullied, for example, will know what to do and who to speak to so that the problem can be dealt with.

Response 2: Low level response – total 3/8 marks

Samira should treat all the children the same and provide activities that all of the children can take part in. All children should be allowed to take part in an activity and none should be excluded, for example because of a disability. She should also make sure that the staff are treating all the children equally. All children should be given a fair chance at an activity. Children who do not speak English should have help to understand what everyone is doing so that they can join in as well.

Now test yourself answers at **www.hoddereducation.co.uk/myrevisionnotes**

Commentary

Question context and requirements:

- The scenario context is a primary school headteacher.
- A 'description' of how to apply the early years value of care 'ensuring equality of opportunity' is required. A list will not gain many marks; some detail is needed.
- This is a 'Levels of response' (LOR) question that requires an extended response. You gain marks for the quality of your description, which should demonstrate your knowledge and understanding of the topic.
- This question is assessed against LO2: Understand the importance of the values of care and how they are applied.

Response 1: 8/8 marks

- The whole answer clearly relates to the context.
- There is good use of appropriate terminology throughout, such as 'access', 'impairments', 'disabilities', 'BSL', 'meet individual needs' and 'policies'.
- The answer is well organised into two paragraphs, each covering a different aspect of ensuring equal opportunities. The first paragraph covers many different aspects of providing access for all. The second paragraph relates directly to the role of headteacher, giving an overview of policies and providing staff training.
- A range of examples is provided to develop the detail of the description.
- All of the information is accurate, relevant and detailed, as required for Level 3.

Response 2: 3/8 marks

- This is a basic response that provides only a limited description.
- There is a lack of specific detail of how to ensure equal opportunities, for example, there are no examples of ways to promote access, such as ramps.
- The answer starts with an inaccurate statement: 'Samira should treat all the children the same'; this does not ensure equal opportunities, as some children may need extra help to achieve or to take part.
- There are several vague statements which are valid and gained credit in Level 1, but lack the detail required to gain higher marks, such as 'none should be excluded, for example because of a disability'; 'make sure that the staff are treating all the children equally'; 'all children should be given a fair chance at an activity'; 'children who do not speak English should have help'. Detail about the type of help needed or how to provide access would have gained more marks.

Mark scheme

Possible answer content:	Levels of response:
Access: • ensure individual access needs are met, e.g. physical access such as ramps or adjustable height tables for wheelchair users • activities adapted or resources adapted, e.g. coloured paper for dyslexia, large print for visual impairment, staff who know BSL, provision for those with English as a second language.	**Level 3 (7–8 marks)** Response provides a detailed description of two or more ways Samira could ensure equality of opportunity at the primary school. Answers will be coherent and well organised, using correct terminology.

Possible answer content:	Levels of response:
Challenge discrimination: • no sexist, racist comments allowed • procedures for challenging discrimination in place • staff trained in equal opportunities and diversity.	**Level 2 (4–6 marks)** Response provides a sound description of at least two ways that equality of opportunity could be applied in a primary school. Answers will be factually correct, using some correct terminology, but may need developing.
Organisational policies: • equal opportunities • bullying.	**Sub-max of 4 marks** for only one way, done well.
Fair treatment: • all children given the same opportunities • differences valued, e.g. race, gender, religion, ethnicity. Accept other appropriate ways. Level 1 for vague responses such as: • treating children equally • letting them all have equal chances. Do not accept: • 'treating all children the same'.	**Level 1 (1–3 marks)** Response provides a basic description of how equality of opportunity could be applied in a primary school. One relevant way or several ways that lack detail and may be listed. Limited use of terminology.

Section A: Sample question 3

James is the Manager of Sunset Retirement Home. He has carried out a review and has found that security is not as good as it should be. He introduces two new security measures to help protect the residents:

1 receiving and monitoring visitors

2 monitoring of keys.

Explain how the two security measures could protect residents at Sunset Retirement Home. [6 marks]

Response 1: High level response – total 6/6 marks

1 Receiving and monitoring visitors:
Having a member of staff on duty at a reception desk by the main entrance would mean that the receptionist could control who is allowed in and out of the retirement home. Visitors would be given a visitor badge so they can be identified as an authorised visitor. This would prevent strangers or intruders from just walking in. It would also prevent any vulnerable residents wandering out unsupervised.

2 Monitoring of keys:
This would keep track of where all the keys are at all times. If a set was lost this would be known straightaway and the locks could be changed to prevent anyone unauthorised, such as a burglar, from entering the building. It limits access to the retirement home to those people who are authorised; the rest would have to report to reception.

Response 2: Low level response – total 3/6 marks

1 Receiving and monitoring visitors:
Giving visitors badges and making them sign in at the desk would protect residents from strangers coming into the home.

2 Monitoring of keys:
So that no one unauthorised can get hold of a set of keys for the retirement home. This keeps residents safe.

Now test yourself answers at **www.hoddereducation.co.uk/myrevisionnotes**

Commentary

Question requirements:

- The scenario context is a retirement home. Answers should be relevant to this type of setting.
- An 'explanation' is required, so you need to include detail about the relevant reasons for and effects of the two security measures.
- This is a points-based question with three marks available for each security measure. So you need to include three bits of information in each answer to gain full marks.
- This question is assessed against LO4: Understand how personal hygiene, safety and security measures protect individuals.

Response 1: 6/6 marks

- This response clearly focuses on the two security measures and how they protect the retirement home residents, relating well to the context.
- All of the information stated is factually correct and demonstrates good knowledge of security measures.
- In each answer there is a concise and detailed explanation of how the security measure would work and specific examples of how this would protect the residents.

Response 2: 3/6 marks

- The answers given show some knowledge of the security measures.
- Some explanation is attempted but is lacking in detail or development.
- In the first answer examples are given – visitor badges and signing in – and protecting residents from strangers is given as a reason. This gains two marks. The answer requires development to gain the third mark. How the security measure would prevent strangers entering is not explained.
- The second answer gains one mark for a statement of fact that unauthorised individuals would not be able to get hold of the keys. No further explanation or reason is provided.

Mark scheme

Security measure:	How residents are protected:
Receiving and monitoring visitors [3 marks]	<ul><li>a member of staff will be on duty at the reception desk</li><li>controls access to the building</li><li>monitors staff and visitors accessing the building</li><li>only allows authorised individuals to enter the care setting</li><li>restricts access to authorised people</li><li>prevents vulnerable service users wandering out of the care setting.</li></ul>
Monitoring of keys [3 marks]	<ul><li>a limited number of people will have keys so access is controlled</li><li>having a list of 'key holders' ensures the whereabouts of all sets of keys is known at all times</li><li>will know straightaway if any keys go missing so action can be taken</li><li>prevents intruders/strangers from entering the building.</li></ul>

Section B: Fact- and knowledge-based questions

Section B: Sample question 1

Identify four protected characteristics named by the Equality Act 2010.

[4 marks]

Response 1: High level response – total 4/4 marks

1 Gender reassignment

2 Pregnancy and maternity

3 Race

4 Sex

Response 2: Low level response – total 1/4 marks

- Race
- Vulnerable adults
- Religion
- Gender, sexual orientation

Commentary

Question requirements:

- Identification of four correct protected characteristics. One mark each.
- This question is assessed against LO3.

Response 1: 4/4 marks

- The four characteristics named are all correct.

Response 2: 1/4 marks

- 'Race' is correct
- 'Vulnerable adults' is not a protected characteristic, so does not gain a mark.
- 'Religion' is incomplete and so does not gain a mark. It should be 'religion or belief'
- 'Gender' is incomplete 'it should be 'gender reassignment'. So does not gain a mark.
- Though correct, 'sexual orientation' does not gain a mark as it is the second answer on the line. Only the first answer given is marked.

Mark scheme

Equality Act 2010, protected characteristics	
- Age	- Race
- Disability	- Religion or belief
- Gender reassignment	- Sex
- Marriage and civil partnership	- Sexual orientation.
- Pregnancy and maternity	

Now test yourself answers at **www.hoddereducation.co.uk/myrevisionnotes**

Section B: Sample question 2

Describe ways that a social care worker could promote and value diversity in care settings.   [8 marks]

Response 1: High level response – total 8/8 marks

A social care worker should find out about the individual cultural needs of the service users, such as if they need a special vegetarian diet or can only be looked after by a female care assistant. This will allow the correct type of care to be provided for each individual and so value the diverse needs of all the individuals in the care setting.

Accepting and providing for the different faiths and religious beliefs held by, for example, residents in a care home, would involve providing access to a prayer room or arranging for a priest to visit. Encouraging all the residents to join in to celebrate Diwali, Eid and not just celebrating Christmas would make everyone feel valued, respected and welcome.

In any care setting a range of adaptations are required to cater for the different needs of individuals, such as leaflets with simplified vocabulary for those with learning disabilities, staff who can sign, hearing loops to cater for those who are hearing impaired, and wide doorways and ramps for wheelchair access. All of these adaptations demonstrate that a care setting values and respects the diversity of the individuals who use their services.

Response 2: Low level response – total 3/8 marks

The ways that staff can promote diversity are by giving choices so no one is left out. Make sure their individual needs are met because everyone is different and has different needs. Do different types of activity for different people.

By having multicultural staff. Serve a range of food from different cultures and celebrate different festivals. Not to treat them any differently because of their race, religion, sexuality or gender.

Commentary

Question requirements:

- A 'description' of ways to promote and value diversity in care settings is required, so relevant facts, features, qualities or aspects of promoting diversity are needed.

- A list will not gain many marks; some detail or examples are needed to develop the answer.

- This question is assessed against LO2: Understand the importance of the values of care and how they are applied.

Response 1: 8/8 marks

- A comprehensive knowledge and understanding of diversity is demonstrated.

- This response is very well organised. The three paragraphs each focus on different aspects of promoting and valuing diversity: the first paragraph focuses on cultural needs; the second on faith and religion; the third on adaptations to meet individual needs.

- This response provides a coherent and detailed description of a range of ways to promote and value diversity.
- A range of examples is provided to develop the detail of the description.
- All of the information is accurate, relevant and detailed, as required for Level 3.

Response 2: 3/8 marks

- The response shows some correct knowledge of promoting and valuing diversity. Some relevant points are given, such as meeting individual needs, different activities, celebrating different festivals, serving a range of food, and so on. However, none of these suggestions are developed.
- Overall the response is 'list-like', which puts it into Level 1. With some development of the points with examples, this response could move into Level 2.
- The response is not completely accurate, as it ends with a statement 'not to treat anyone differently', which is contradictory. This aspect needs to be better described.

Mark scheme

Ways of promoting and valuing diversity	Additional description and examples	Levels of response
Equal and fair treatment **Non-discriminatory behaviour** **Meeting individual needs** **Valuing diversity**	All individuals treated fairly irrespective of age, race, gender, religion, disability, ethnicity, sexuality, and so on. All individuals given the same choices and opportunities regardless of differences, such as visits arranged to places with wheelchair access/hearing loop, etc. Care workers will not: • be patronising • exclude individuals • discriminate against individuals due to differences such as race, gender, religion, age, disability, sexuality and so on. If a care worker witnesses any discriminatory behaviour, it would be reported and challenged with the individual concerned. Providing for dietary, cultural, religious, mobility and communication needs; for example, meal options include diabetic, gluten free, vegetarian, halal, kosher and so on. Meet cultural and religious requirements, such as female care assistant/nurse/GP. Ensuring all areas and resources are accessible to all – through provision of ramps, automatic doors, hearing loop, information in different formats and languages, staff who can sign and so on. Care workers will: • accept and respect individual differences, for example, faith, language, diet, customs, and so on • provide activities, resources, food reflecting different cultures, beliefs, faiths • celebrate a range of festivals, for example, Eid, Chinese New Year, Easter and so on.	**Level 3 (7–8 marks)** Response provides a detailed description of at least two ways of promoting and valuing diversity in care settings. Answers will be factually correct, coherent and use correct terminology. **Level 2 (4–6 marks)** Response provides a sound explanation of one or two ways of promoting and valuing diversity. Some reference to care settings. Some correct terminology will be used. **Sub-max of 4 marks** for one way, done well. **Level 1 (1–3 marks)** Response provides way(s) of promoting and valuing diversity. One relevant way or several ways that lack detail and may be list-like. Limited use of terminology.

Section B: Sample question 3

Outline key aspects of the Health and Safety at Work Act 1974 that apply to service providers and practitioners.

Your answer should include:

- aspects of the Act that apply to service providers
- aspects of the Act that apply to care practitioners. [6 marks]

Response 1: High level response – total 6/6 marks

The main aspects of the Health and Safety at Work Act for service providers are that they have the duty to provide a safe place to work. They have a duty to carry out risk assessments and reduce any risks that are identified. They must protect the service users so the building should be safe, secure and hygienic. According to HASAWA the service provider has to give any PPE (protective clothing) needed to the staff free of charge and provide health and safety training. The service provider must provide a written health and safety policy.

The main aspects of the Health and Safety at Work Act for practitioners are that if they find something that is a risk, for example a faulty hoist, they have a duty to report it because they are responsible for their own safety and that of others. HASAWA also states that they must also wear any protective clothing they are provided with and follow all safety procedures that are in place at the care setting, such as fire procedures and not using any equipment that they have not received training for.

Response 2: Low level response – total 3/6 marks

Service providers must check each piece of equipment is tested regularly to ensure that it is safe and staff will need to be given training in order to use the equipment safely. If there are machines that are dangerous the correct PPE should be provided such as goggles. The service provider should make sure that there are fire procedures for practitioners to follow and make sure they are given training in the procedures.

Commentary

Question requirements:

- An 'outline' is required, so you need to give the key facts about the Health and Safety at Work Act.
- Aspects that apply to **both** service providers and practitioners must be included in your answer. It is a good idea to write a separate paragraph for each to give a balanced answer.
- This is a 'Levels of response' (LOR) question that requires an extended response. You gain marks for the quality of your outline, which should demonstrate your knowledge and understanding of the Health and Safety at Work Act.
- This question is assessed against LO3: Understand how legislation impacts on care settings.

Response 1: 6/6 marks

- This response is well organised with two paragraphs, one focusing on service providers and the other on practitioners. This ensures that requirements for both groups of people are covered, which is a demand of the question.
- All of the information about the Health and Safety at Work Act is factually correct.
- In each paragraph an outline is given of several aspects of the Act. This satisfies the question requirement of 'aspect**s**', which is plural so you must give a minimum of two.
- There is good use of terminology, such as 'risk assessments', 'protective clothing', 'duty to report' and 'safety procedures'.
- The answer clearly demonstrates knowledge and understanding of the Act.
- All the information is accurate, relevant and in sufficient detail for an 'outline'.

Response 2: 3/6 marks

- The answer shows correct knowledge of aspects of the HASAWA.
- Some correct terminology is used, such as PPE, safety procedures, training.
- More than one aspect of HASAWA requirements that apply to service providers are covered in the answer: testing equipment to check it is safe, PPE and training for using equipment and for fire procedures.
- Only requirements of the aspects relating to service providers are given. This limits the answer to Level 1, as the question demands that aspects of the Act that apply to both service providers *and* practitioners are given. For Level 2 marks, the answer must include at least one aspect of HASAWA relating to service providers and one aspect for practitioners, and so this answer does not meet the criteria for Level 2.

Mark scheme

The Health and Safety at Work Act:	Levels of response:
Key aspects for service providers • They must ensure that the working environment does not put workers, service users or visitors at risk. • The equipment provided must be safe and in good working order. • Health and safety training must be provided for all staff. • There must be a written health and safety policy. • Free of charge protective equipment, if needed, must be available for employees.	**Level 2 (5–6 marks)** Response provides a clear outline of two or more aspects of the legislation. Answers include at least one aspect relating to service providers *and* one aspect for practitioners. Answers are factually correct, coherent and well organised, using correct terminology.
Key aspects for practitioners • They must co-operate with their employer by following health and safety regulations in the care setting. • They have a duty to report any hazards to their employer. • They must not misuse or tamper with equipment that meets health and safety regulations, e.g. fire extinguishers. • They have a responsibility to take care of themselves and others in the workplace.	**Level 1 (1–4 marks)** Response provides a sound outline of two or more relevant aspects of the legislation that are, in the main, factually correct. May provide limited information about several aspects. At the lower end of this level the response may be list-like and demonstrate little use of terminology.

Glossary

Advocate: someone who speaks on behalf of an individual who is unable to speak up for him or herself.

Anaphylactic shock: an extreme allergic reaction. Common causes can be nuts, celery, seafood, and wasp or bee stings.

Anti-bacterial: something that destroys bacteria or prevents their growth.

Bacteria: tiny, microscopic organisms. Some bacteria can cause infection and disease.

Body language: a type of non-verbal communication through body posture, facial expressions, gestures and eye contact.

Breach: breaking the law; not meeting the requirements.

BSL: British Sign Language. A communication system of hand movements, gestures, body language and facial expressions used by those who are deaf or have a hearing impairment. Also used by non-deaf people to assist with effective communication.

Cannulas: thin tubes that surround a flexible needle that is inserted into a vein to administer medication from a drip.

Care setting: anywhere that care is provided. Different care settings provide different types of care.

Confidentiality: limits access or places restrictions on sharing certain types of sensitive information, so that it is kept private to only those who need to be aware of it.

Consultation: the process of discussing something with someone in order to get his or her advice or opinion, so that a decision can be made that is acceptable to all involved.

Contamination: when something is tainted with other substances that may be unclean; for example, disease-causing bacteria.

Control measures: actions that can be taken to reduce the risks posed by hazards or to remove hazards altogether.

Cross-contamination: when bacteria spreads onto food from another source, such as hands, work surfaces, kitchen equipment and utensils, or between cooked and raw food.

DBS checks: criminal record checks carried out by the Disclosure and Barring Service (DBS), to help prevent unsuitable people working with vulnerable adults or children.

Designated protection officer: this person provides information and support to staff in care settings in relation to disclosures and suspicions of abuse. Early years settings have a 'designated child protection officer'.

Direct discrimination: intentionally putting someone at a disadvantage or treating them unfairly based on their differences, i.e., their 'protected characteristics'.

Disability: a physical or mental impairment that limits a person's movement, senses or activities.

Disciplinary action: a member of staff may be given a warning, or suspended or – in very serious circumstances – dismissed because of not doing their job properly to the required standards.

Discrimination: the unjust and unfair treatment of individuals based on their differences, such as race, religious beliefs, disability or gender.

Disempowerment: feeling that you have a lack of control over your life and lack independence.

Diversity: the recognition that everyone is different and has different needs, so appreciating and respecting individual differences such as a person's choice of faith, diet, ethnicity and customs.

Dynavox: speech-generating software. By touching a screen that contains text, pictures and symbols, the software then converts those symbols touched into speech.

Employees: practitioners, care workers and other staff in a care setting.

Empowerment: the process that enables individuals to take control of their lives and make their own decisions. Giving someone confidence in their own abilities.

Epipen: an emergency treatment for someone with severe anaphylactic reaction. It is an automatic injector device that contains a dose of the hormone adrenaline, which is injected into the thigh.

Equality: enabling individuals to have the same rights, access and opportunities as everyone else regardless of gender, race, ability, age, sexual orientation or religious belief.

Gender reassignment: when a person's physical sexual characteristics are changed by medical procedures such as surgery or hormone treatment.

Gluten free: a diet that does not include the grains wheat, barley and rye, which can trigger a dietary intolerance in some individuals.

GP: a General Practitioner, the doctor you go to see at your local surgery.

Halal: a diet in which no pork is eaten and all meat has to be prepared according to Muslim law.

Harassment: unwanted behaviour that intends to intimidate or humiliate someone.

Hazard: anything that could cause harm.

Hearing loop: a special type of sound system for use by people with hearing aids. It provides a wireless signal that is picked up by the hearing aid and can greatly improve the quality of sound.

Hospice: a setting that provides support and end-of-life care to individuals and their families.

Hygiene: practices that keep you and your surroundings clean in order to prevent illness and the spread of disease.

Indirect discrimination: when a policy, practice or a rule applies to everybody but has a detrimental effect on some people. For example, a job advert that states male applicants must be clean-shaven would discriminate against individuals who grow facial hair because of their religious beliefs.

Infection: when germs and bacteria invade the body and cause a disease or illness.

Interpreter: converts a spoken or signed message from one language to another.

Jargon: specialist or technical language or terms and abbreviations that are difficult for non-specialists to understand.

Kosher: in Judaism, this is used to describe something that is 'correct'; that is, food is sold, cooked or eaten satisfying the requirements of Jewish law. Meat and dairy cannot be eaten at the same meal.

Learned helplessness: when someone gives up trying as a result of consistent lack of achievement or reward – they come to believe that it is not worth trying because they will fail anyway.

Legislation: a collection of laws passed by Parliament, which state the rights and entitlements of the individual. Law is upheld through the courts.

Lightwriter: a text-to-speech device. A message is typed on a keyboard, displayed on a screen and then converted into speech.

Manual handling: using the correct procedures when physically moving any load by lifting, putting down, pushing or pulling.

Marginalised: excluded from participating; feeling unimportant and not wanted by the majority of people.

Mental capacity: the ability to make decisions (by understanding information and remembering it for long enough) and communicate them to others.

Monitoring: to measure and check the progress or quality of something over time. Methods of monitoring can involve observations, inspections, analysis or service user questionnaires.

Need-to-know basis: information is only shared with those directly involved with the care and support of an individual.

Neglect: fail to look after properly.

Paramountcy principle: the child's best interest and welfare is the first and most important consideration.

Patronising: talking down to someone, as though they were a child or simple-minded.

PAT testing: Portable Appliance Testing is the term used to describe the checking of electrical appliances and equipment to ensure they are safe to use.

PECS: Stands for 'Picture Exchange Communication System'. It is a specialist method of communication developed for use with children who have autism. It helps them learn to start communicating by exchanging a picture for the item or activity they want.

PPE: personal protective equipment provided by your employer. This is any clothing and protective equipment designed to ensure personal safety in the workplace.

Prejudice: a dislike of, or negative attitude towards, an individual often based on ill-informed personal opinion. Examples include racial prejudice and homophobia.

Proactive: taking action intended to cause changes rather than just reacting to the situation after it has happened.

Redress: to obtain justice after receiving inadequate care. This may take the form of compensation awarded by the courts or having your rights restored in some way.

Reflective practitioner: someone who regularly looks back at the work they do, and how they do it, to consider how they can improve their practice.

Risk: the likelihood that someone or something could be harmed.

Risk assessment: the process of evaluating the likelihood of a hazard actually causing harm.

Safeguarding: measures taken to reduce the risks of danger, harm and abuse.

Security measures: all the actions taken within a care setting to protect individuals; for example, procedures to ensure that only people with permission enter or leave the building.

Sensory impairment: when one of the senses (sight, hearing, smell, touch, taste and spatial awareness) does not function normally. For example, if you wear glasses you have sight impairment; if you wear a hearing aid then you have a hearing impairment.

Sexual orientation: an individual's sexual preferences; for example, homosexual or heterosexual.

Sharps: items of equipment with sharp points that can puncture or cut the skin; examples include needles and cannulas.

Sharps injury: when the skin is punctured by a needle or blade, such as a scalpel or other medical instrument.

Social care: the provision of personal care, protection or support services for children and adults in need or at risk. Needs may arise from illness, disability, old age or poverty. Social care involves practical support with personal and daily living tasks and emotional support where necessary, as well as providing protection services for children or adults in need or at risk of harm.

Special educational needs: children with learning or physical disabilities, for example, hearing or visual impairments, or conditions such as ADHD or autism.

Tone: the strength of a vocal sound made, for example, quiet or loud.

Translator: converts a written message from one language to another.

Victimisation: bad treatment directed towards someone who has made a complaint or has taken action under the Equality Act or other legislation.

Vulnerable: someone who is less able to protect themselves from harm due to, for example, mental health problems or a physical or learning disability.

Whistle blowing: when someone reveals serious wrongdoing within an organisation to an outside authority such as the Care Quality Commission, so that it can be investigated.

Photo credits

The Publishers would like to thank the following for permission to reproduce copyright material.

p8 © Civil / Shutterstock; p10 © create jobs 51 / Shutterstock; p14 © DGLimages / Shutterstock; p16 © Cathy Yeulet / 123RF; p17 © Cathy Yeulet / 123RF; p19 © Dean Mitchell/deanm1974/Fotolia.com; p21 © Monkey Business Images – Shutterstock; p26 © WavebreakMediaMicro / stock.adobe.com; p30 © Cathy Yeulet / 123RF; p34 © Igor Zakowski / Shutterstock; p39 © radub85/123RF ; p40 © Photographee.eu / Shutterstock; p50 *tl* © marcos calvo mesa / 123RF, *tc* © Cathy Yeulet / 123RF *tr* © obencem / 123RF, *bl* © Bela Hoche / 123RF, *bc* © Katarzyna Białasiewicz / 123RF, *br* © MaszaS / 123RF; p55 © Teguh Mujiono / 123RF; p60 © Africa Studio / Shutterstock; p66© Crown Copyright; p68 © Tyler Olson / stock.adobe/com; p69 © Monkey Business Images / Shutterstock; p70 © kunertus / stock.adobe.com; p72 © NPCC; p74 *l* © BSI Group, *c* © The British Toy & Hobby Association, *r* © European Commission; p76 © John Birdsall / Alamy Stock Photo; p77 © John Birdsall / Alamy Stock Photo; p80 © Phanie / Alamy Stock Photo; p81 © Andrey Popov / stock.adobe.com; p83 © Andrew Callaghan ; p87 © tigatelu / stock.adobe.com.

Every effort has been made to trace all copyright holders, but if any have been inadvertently overlooked, the Publishers will be pleased to make the necessary arrangements at the first opportunity.